D1101738

ST. HELENS LIBRARIES

3 8055 35036 0533

BEANO.

BOOK OF

MISCHIEF, MAYHEM & FUN

St.Helens Library Services	
3805535036053	
PETERS	17-Sep-2018
790.194	£14.99

Studio Press
An imprint of Kings Road Publishing
Part of Bonnier Publishing
The Plaza, 535 King's Road,
London, SW10 0SZ
www.studiopressbooks.co.uk
www.beano.com

A Beano Studios Product © D.C. Thomson & Co. Ltd 2018

Edited by Matt Yeo
Designed by Grant Kempster
Packaged by Cloud King Creative

All rights reserved. No part of this publication may be
reproduced or transmitted in any form or by any means,
electronic or mechanical, including photocopying, recording,
or any information storage and retrieval system,
without written permission in writing from the publisher.

A CIP catalogue record for this book
is available from the British Library.

Flexiback: 978-1-78741-161-6
Printed in Italy
2 4 6 8 10 9 7 5 3 1

Studio Press is an imprint of Bonnier Publishing Company
www.bonnierpublishing.co.uk

BEANO
BOOK OF
MISCHIEF, MAYHEM & FUN

STUDIO PRESS

CONTENTS
INDOOR FUN

CREATIVE FUN

OUTDOOR FUN

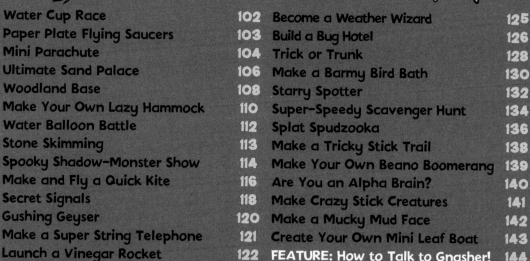

SPORTS & GAMES

ESSENTIAL MISCHIEF-MAKING KIT

You'll need lots of different of things to make, build, create and play all of the awesome activities in this book. Here's a list of some of the most important items to grab from around your house!

Scissors
Sticky Tape
Coloured Markers
Wax Crayons
Ruler
Pencils
Pens
Rubber
Paints
Paintbrushes
Masking Tape
Paper
Thick and Thin Cardboard
Cardboard Tubes
Craft Knife
Wire Cutters
Rubber Bands
Plastic Spoons
Paper Plates
Strong Glue

Fabric Glue
Socks
Buttons
Googly Eyes
Pipe Cleaners
Glitter
Plastic Bottles
Water
Food Colouring
Torch
Cotton Buds
String
Newspaper
Bottle Tops
Kitchen Towels
Cotton Thread
Eggs
Camera
Paper Clips
Drinking Straws
Ziplock Sandwich Bags
Modelling Clay
Plastic Funnel
Cotton Wool
Balloons
Craft Sticks
Plastic Cups
Bucket
An Adult
Your Friends!

INDOOR FUN!

Stuck indoors on a rainy day? Bored out of your mind with nothing to do? Then have we got some cool treats for you! Don't let the rubbish weather outside put you off – you can still be a mega Menace inside with our handy trick, prank and gag ideas. Grab what you need and let the mischief begin!

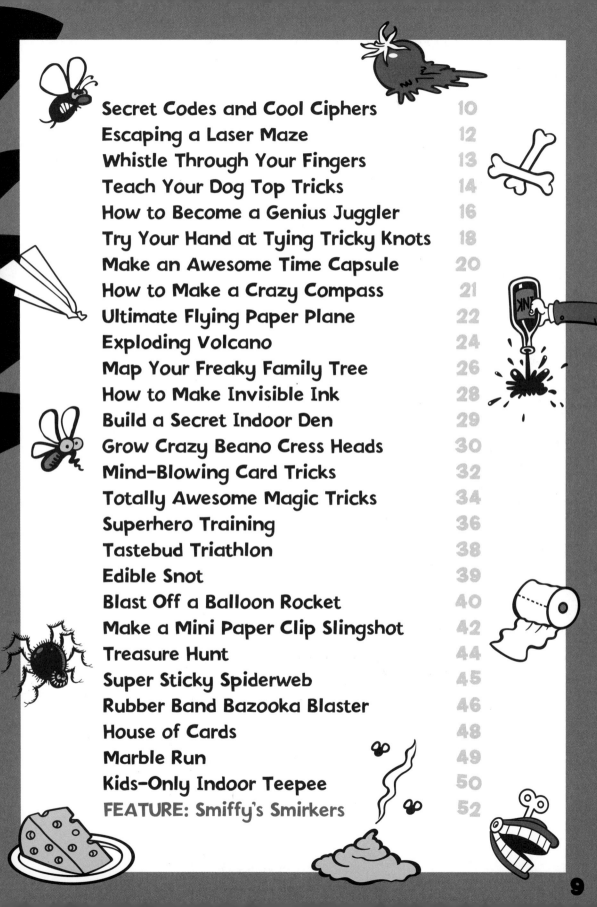

SECRET CODES AND
COOL CIPHERS

MORSE CODE

Use these codes and ciphers to send
super-secret messages to your mates!

In **MORSE CODE**, letters and numbers are shown as dots and dashes:

A:	• —		**J:**	• — — —		**S:**	• • •
B:	— • • •		**K:**	— • —		**T:**	—
C:	• — • —		**L:**	• — • •		**U:**	• • —
D:	— • •		**M:**	— —		**V:**	• • • —
E:	•		**N:**	— •		**W:**	• — —
F:	• • — •		**O:**	— — —		**X:**	— • • —
G:	— — •		**P:**	• — — •		**Y:**	— • — —
H:	• • • •		**Q:**	— — • —		**Z:**	— — • •
I:	• •		**R:**	• — •			

QUICK BEANO CODES

Use the Morse Code key above to see if you can work out what these
four secret Beano Morse Code messages REALLY say:

—•• •— —•• / ••• —— • •—•• •—•• •••

•• / •—• ——— •—•— —•—

—••• •— —•/ ••• •—•— •••• ——— ——— •—••

—••• • •— —• ——— / •—• ••— •—•• • •••

ROT1

ROT1 is a clever and simple cipher.

Each letter of the alphabet is replaced with the letter that follows. So A is replaced with B, B is replaced with C and so on.

"ROT1" means "rotate 1 letter forwards through the alphabet". Cool!

The words "MISCHIEF, MAYHEM AND FUN" would become "NJTDIJFG, NBZIFN BOE GVO"!

Can you work out this ROT1 coded message? "J MPWF UIF CFBOP!"

ER... WHY DID I WRITE ALL OF MY HOMEWORK ANSWERS IN A TRICKY CODE?

THE CAESAR SHIFT CIPHER

You only need to know which Caesar cipher was used in order to decipher a message. If the G cipher is used, then A becomes G, B becomes H, C becomes I and so on through the alphabet.

If the Y CIPHER is used, then A becomes Y, B becomes Z, C becomes A and so on. Use this cipher to make sure all of your sneaky notes in class stay super-secret!

The CAESAR SHIFT CIPHER, is so-called because it was used by Emperor Julius Caesar himself. It's actually 26 different ciphers, one for each letter of the alphabet!

QUICK BEANO CODES:
DAD SMELLS
I ROCK
BAN SCHOOL
BEANO RULES
ROT1 CIPHER: I LOVE THE BEANO!

ESCAPING A
LASER MAZE

Sneaking through a maze of laser beams is easy for a true Menace!

YOU WILL NEED:
- RIBBON (OR WOOL OR ELASTIC)
- A ROOM WITH PLENTY OF ANCHOR POINTS

1 FIRST, FIND A ROOM THAT'S NOT TOO WIDE, WITH SAFE PLACES TO TIE YOUR RIBBON. A HALLWAY IS GOOD BECAUSE THERE ARE USUALLY LOTS OF HANDY DOOR HANDLES!

2 ZIGZAG THE RIBBON ACROSS THE ROOM, HIGH AND LOW. LOOP IT AROUND DOORKNOBS, BOXES, CHAIR LEGS AND THE BOTTOM OF A BANNISTER. JUST AVOID HEAVY FURNITURE THAT MIGHT TOPPLE OVER OR THE TOP OF A STAIRCASE, WHERE SOMEONE COULD TRIP.

3 ASK AN ADULT TO CHECK THAT IT'S SAFE BEFORE YOU START TO PLAY. (ADULTS ARE USEFUL FOR TYING THE RIBBON TO HIGH ANCHOR POINTS, TOO.) NOW, WEAVE YOUR WAY THROUGH THE LASER MAZE WITHOUT TOUCHING THE RIBBON!

TOP TIP:
Attach small bells to the ribbons so the slightest touch will sound an alarm!

HE, HE! I SNUCK THIS BAG OF WORMS UNDER MY DAD'S BED!

WHISTLE THROUGH
YOUR FINGERS

Every Menace needs to be able to do this, so that you can call your mates with a quick whistle. Here's how!

 1 HOLD YOUR MIDDLE AND INDEX FINGERS TOGETHER ON EACH HAND, AND USE THE THUMB TO HOLD BACK THE OTHER TWO FINGERS. EASY!

 2 WET YOUR LIPS A LITTLE AND DRAW THEM OVER YOUR TEETH LIKE YOU'RE PRETENDING TO BE A TOOTHLESS OLD MAN! MAKE SURE TO KEEP YOUR TEETH COVERED BY YOUR LIPS WHEN YOU WHISTLE.

 3 PLACE YOUR FINGERS UNDERNEATH THE VERY TIP OF YOUR TONGUE. TASTY!

 4 USING YOUR FINGERS, PUSH BACK YOUR TONGUE UNTIL THE FIRST KNUCKLES (JUST BELOW YOUR FINGERNAILS) ON YOUR FINGERS REACH YOUR BOTTOM LIP.

 5 CLOSE YOUR LIPS TIGHTLY ROUND YOUR FINGERS WITH NO GAPS, OTHER THAN THE LITTLE HOLE BETWEEN YOUR FINGERS TO LET THE WHISTLE OUT. NOW BLOW HARD!

TEACH YOUR DOG

TOP TRICKS

Train your dog to help you with your sneaky Menacing plans!

TOP TRAINING TIPS:

1. Keep commands to one or two simple words, which will be easier for your dog to recognise.
2. Keep training sessions short – five minutes will do.
3. Your dog will learn tricks more easily if their training session ends well. If the five minutes are almost up and your dog is doing something well, stop there and give them a scrummy treat!

YOU WILL NEED:
- A DOG
- A CLICKER
- DOG TREATS

TRAIN YOUR DOG TO ...

SIT

 1 WAIT UNTIL YOUR DOG SITS DOWN ON ITS OWN. USE THE CLICKER AND GIVE THEM A TREAT.

 2 REPEAT. IF YOUR DOG IS LIKE GNASHER, THEY'LL PROBABLY JUST SCARPER WITH THE TREATS!

 3 SAY "SIT" AS SOON AS THEY SIT. USE THE CLICKER AND GIVE THEM A TREAT.

 4 REPEAT.

 5 SAY "SIT". IF THEY SIT, CLICK AND GIVE THEM A TASTY TREAT!

COME

 1 CHOOSE A WORD TO USE TO MAKE YOUR DOG COME TO YOU.

 2 GO TO YOUR DOG AND USE THAT WORD, THEN TREAT THEM. NOM, NOM...

 3 REPEAT DURING THE DAY, GIVING A DIFFERENT TREAT EACH TIME AND LOADS OF PRAISE.

 4 GO ACROSS THE ROOM AND USE THE CUE WORD. WHEN YOUR DOG COMES, CLICK THE CLICKER, PET ITS HEAD AND LOOP YOUR HAND UNDER THEIR COLLAR TO GET THEM USED TO BEING HELD.

 5 GIVE YOUR DOG A TREAT.

 6 TRY CALLING FROM ANOTHER ROOM OR WHEN YOUR DOG IS INTERESTED IN SOMETHING. VARY THE REWARD BETWEEN TREATS PLUS PRAISE, AND JUST PRAISE.

HIGH FIVE, PAW, SHAKE HANDS

1 GET YOUR DOG TO SIT, LIKE GNASHER WHEN HE'S WATCHING TV!

2 WHEN THEY LIFT UP THEIR PAW, PRESS THE CLICKER AND REWARD THEM WITH A TREAT.

3 REPEAT.

4 WAIT FOR THEM TO LIFT THEIR PAW, HOWEVER SLIGHTLY, THEN CLICK AND TREAT.

5 SAY "PAW" WHENEVER THEY LIFT THEIR PAW.

6 START TREATING ONLY WHEN THEY LIFT THEIR PAW HIGHER.

KISS

1 PLACE SOMETHING TASTY ON YOUR CHEEK, LIKE A BISCUIT OR DOGGY CHOCOLATE.

2 USE THE CUE WORD "KISS".

3 LEAN TOWARDS YOUR DOG AND THEY SHOULD LICK THE TREAT FROM YOUR CHEEK. GROSS!

4 REPEAT UNTIL THEY RESPOND TO THE CUE WITHOUT THE YUMMY TREAT.

NICE ONE, GNASHER! NOW I'LL TEACH YOU HOW TO ROCK OUT, LIKE ME!

DID YOU KNOW?

Dogs belong to the canine family, which includes coyotes, foxes, jackals and wolves!

HOW TO BECOME A
GENIUS JUGGLER

Juggling is a seriously cool skill for show-offs. With just a little focus, practice and rhythm, you can really impress your mates!

SAFETY FIRST!

Don't go trying to juggle with flaming torches. You're sure to burn your eyebrows off and then you won't look so cool!

1 FIND A SPACE, THEN GRAB A SMALL BALL OR BEANBAG. TOSS IT FROM ONE HAND TO THE OTHER IN AN ARC – NO HIGHER THAN EYE LEVEL. EASY, RIGHT?

DID YOU KNOW?

One of your hands is called the dominant hand because it does most of the throwing and catching. It's usually the hand you write with!

2 NOW TOSS THE BALL FROM ONE HAND TO THE OTHER, WITHOUT REACHING OUT TO GRAB IT. PRACTICE UNTIL YOU'VE GOT A GOOD RHYTHM GOING.

 3 TRY TOSSING TWO BALLS AT ONCE. AS THE FIRST BALL IS COMING DOWN, THROW THE SECOND BALL AND THEN CATCH BOTH.

 4 ADD A THIRD BALL, SO YOU'RE HOLDING THREE IN TOTAL. YOUR DOMINANT HAND SHOULD BE HOLDING TWO OF THE BALLS.

 5 THROW THE FIRST TWO BALLS JUST AS BEFORE, HOLDING THE THIRD BALL IN YOUR DOMINANT HAND.

 6 ADD A THIRD THROW, JUST WHEN THE SECOND BALL IS AT ITS PEAK, AND KEEP THROWING THE BALLS IN A CONTINUOUS LOOP. TRICKY!

TOP TIP:
Why not try juggling with a few tomatoes? They make a great mess if you drop them!

TRY YOUR HAND AT TYING
TRICKY KNOTS

Knowing how to tie knots can come in handy for all sorts of brilliant pranks. Take a look at these three nifty knots!

SQUARE KNOT

The square knot is used to tie two ropes together.
It's really useful when setting up sneaky traps!

1 LAY THE LEFT-HAND END OF ONE ROPE OVER THE RIGHT-HAND END OF THE OTHER. PASS THE LEFT-HAND END UNDER THE OTHER ROPE AND PULL IT TO THE TOP.

2 POINT THE ENDS INWARDS. PASS THE RIGHT-HAND ONE OVER THE LEFT, THEN TAKE IT DOWN BEHIND IT AND UP TO THE FRONT, THROUGH THE LOOP THAT'S NOW BEEN FORMED.

3

PULL THE KNOT TIGHT. AN EASY WAY TO REMEMBER HOW TO TIE THIS KNOT IS TO SAY: "LEFT OVER RIGHT AND RIGHT OVER LEFT". EASY!

THEY'RE "KNOT" GOING TO LIKE THIS PRANK!

The bowline is used to form a non-slip loop in the end of a rope.
You'll need to be able to tie one of these knots if you go rock climbing!

FORM A LOOP IN THE ROPE BY PASSING THE WORKING (BOTTOM) PART OF YOUR ROPE UP OVER THE STANDING PART (THE ATTACHED PART).

PASS THE WORKING END BACK UP THROUGH THE LOOP FROM BEHIND AND THEN AROUND THE BACK OF THE STANDING PART.

PASS THE WORKING END BACK DOWN THE LOOP AND PULL TIGHTLY. ALL DONE!

CLOVE HITCH

Use this to tie a rope to the handle of a bucket of water. Place the
bucket above a door and yank the rope when someone walks under it!

 PASS THE WORKING END OVER AND UNDER THE HANDLE. RUN IT ACROSS THE STANDING PART.

 GO ROUND THE HANDLE AGAIN, BRINGING THE WORKING END BACK. TUCK IT UNDER THE CROSS.

 PULL TIGHTLY. THE TWO ENDS OF THE ROPE SHOULD LIE NEXT TO EACH OTHER UNDER THE CROSS, IN OPPOSITE DIRECTIONS.

MAKE AN AWESOME
TIME CAPSULE

Making a time capsule is like creating a cool treasure chest. Select and seal some secret stuff away, ready for future Menaces to dig up and discover!

YOUR CAPSULE

1. Find an airtight box with a lid to make your time capsule.
2. Write the date and your name on the outside of the box, then fill it with all sorts of awesome items!
3. Next, seal it up and hide it somewhere safe, like your loft or cellar, or bury it in the garden. Make sure you remember where you hid it!

TOP TIP:
Put a message in your time capsule telling future kids your best tricks and pranks!

OLD TOYS

MAGAZINES OR COMICS

COOL CLOTHES

WRITE THE DATE AND YOUR NAME ON THE TIME CAPSULE!

SECRET MENACE PLANS

PHOTOS OF YOU AND YOUR MATES.

COINS

HOW TO MAKE A
CRAZY COMPASS

The needle on a compass always points north and could end up leading you to REAL buried treasure!

YOU WILL NEED:

- STRAIGHTENED PAPER CLIP, TO USE AS A NEEDLE
- BAR MAGNET (A RECTANGULAR MAGNET WITH A NORTH AND SOUTH POLE ON EITHER SIDE)
- PLIERS
- ROUND PIECE OF CORK
- SMALL DISH, HALF FILLED WITH WATER

1 FIRST, MAGNETISE YOUR PAPER CLIP NEEDLE BY RUBBING IT FAST AGAINST THE MAGNET ABOUT 20 TIMES, IN THE SAME DIRECTION.

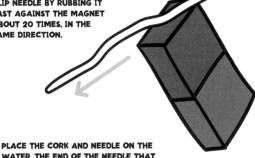

2 GET AN ADULT TO PUSH THE NEEDLE CAREFULLY THROUGH THE CORK USING THE PLIERS. YOU NEED THE SAME AMOUNT OF NEEDLE SHOWING ON EACH SIDE.

3 PLACE THE CORK AND NEEDLE ON THE WATER. THE END OF THE NEEDLE THAT POINTS TOWARDS THE SUN AT MIDDAY IS POINTING SOUTH IF YOU'RE IN THE NORTHERN HEMISPHERE AND NORTH IF YOU'RE IN THE SOUTHERN HEMISPHERE!

UH-OH! LOOKS LIKE I'M LOST AGAIN!

DANGER!

ULTIMATE FLYING
PAPER PLANE

Make perfect paper planes for sending sneaky secret messages to your mates in class!

HOW TO MAKE YOUR OWN PAPER PLANE

1

FOLD THE PAPER IN HALF LENGTHWAYS AND OPEN IT UP AGAIN. EVEN I CAN DO THAT!

2

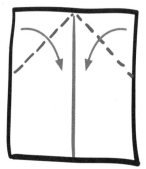

TAKE THE TOP-RIGHT CORNER AND FOLD IT DOWN SO IT MEETS THE CENTRE CREASE. DO THE SAME WITH THE TOP-LEFT CORNER, CHUMS.

3

YOU SHOULD NOW HAVE A TRIANGLE AT THE TOP OF THE PAPER. ER... DID I DO IT RIGHT?

4

NOW FOLD THE TRIANGLE DOWN TOWARDS THE CENTRE OF THE PAPER.

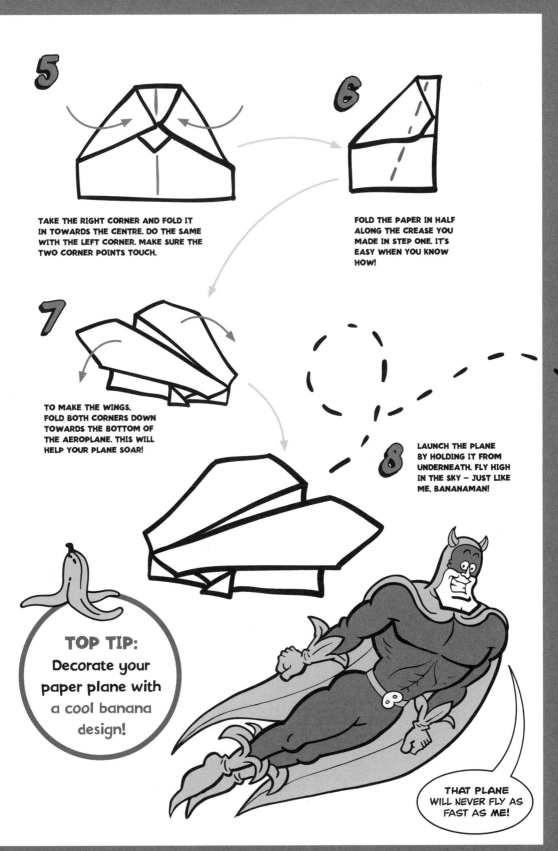

5

TAKE THE RIGHT CORNER AND FOLD IT IN TOWARDS THE CENTRE. DO THE SAME WITH THE LEFT CORNER. MAKE SURE THE TWO CORNER POINTS TOUCH.

6

FOLD THE PAPER IN HALF ALONG THE CREASE YOU MADE IN STEP ONE. IT'S EASY WHEN YOU KNOW HOW!

7

TO MAKE THE WINGS, FOLD BOTH CORNERS DOWN TOWARDS THE BOTTOM OF THE AEROPLANE. THIS WILL HELP YOUR PLANE SOAR!

8

LAUNCH THE PLANE BY HOLDING IT FROM UNDERNEATH. FLY HIGH IN THE SKY – JUST LIKE ME, BANANAMAN!

TOP TIP:
Decorate your paper plane with a cool banana design!

THAT PLANE WILL NEVER FLY AS FAST AS ME!

23

EXPLODING
VOLCANO

Make your own mini volcano at home using just a few items from your kitchen cabinet. Watch out! You'll need to clear plenty of space and ask an adult to help you!

YOU WILL NEED:
- MODELLING CLAY
- 1-LITRE PLASTIC BOTTLE WITH LID
- RED FOOD COLOURING
- WASHING-UP LIQUID
- WHITE VINEGAR
- 30 GRAMS OF BAKING POWDER
- WARM WATER
- PLASTIC FUNNEL
- BAKING TRAY
- A HELPFUL ADULT

1 ON THE BAKING TRAY, PLACE THE MODELLING CLAY AROUND THE PLASTIC BOTTLE TO CREATE A MOUNTAIN SHAPE. LEAVE THE TOP OF THE BOTTLE OPEN AND MAKE SURE NOTHING DROPS INSIDE!

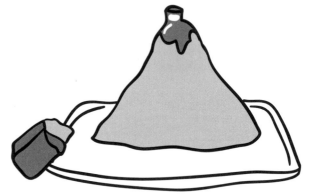

2 MIX A FEW DROPS OF FOOD COLOURING WITH WATER UNTIL IT TURNS A FIERY SHADE OF RED.

3 POUR THE RED LAVA WATER INTO THE MOUNTAIN'S OPENING USING THE PLASTIC FUNNEL.

TOP TIP:
Cover your baking tray with sand and add some toy dinosaurs to make a prehistoric volcano scene!

24

4 ADD SIX DROPS OF THE WASHING-UP LIQUID AND 30 GRAMS OF BAKING POWDER INTO THE MOUNTAIN, TOO.

DID YOU KNOW?
● The word "volcano" comes from the Roman god of fire, Vulcan.
● The largest-known volcano in the universe is Olympus Mons, a volcano on the planet Mars. It measures over 374 miles wide, which is as big as the entire country of Austria!
● One of Jupiter's moons is completely covered in volcanoes!

5 SLOWLY POUR THE WHITE VINEGAR THROUGH THE FUNNEL – YOU WON'T NEED MUCH BEFORE THE LAVA ERUPTION BEGINS. MAKE SURE YOU DON'T STAND WITH YOUR HEAD OVER THE FUNNEL, THOUGH – IN CASE IT ERUPTS RIGHT IN YOUR FACE!

GOTTA RUN! IT'S GONNA BLOW!!

MAP YOUR FREAKY
FAMILY TREE

Ever wondered where your family came from? Maybe you're related to a long line of mischief-makers? Make a family tree and find out!

YOU WILL NEED:
- A LARGE PIECE OF PAPER OR SEVERAL SHEETS TAPED TOGETHER
- STICKY NOTES
- COLOURED PENS OR PENCILS

1 WRITE THE NAMES OF YOUR FAMILY MEMBERS ON STICKY NOTES, SO YOU CAN EASILY MOVE THEM AROUND. LEAVE SPACE AT THE BOTTOM OF EACH NOTE TO FILL IN HOW THEY'RE RELATED TO YOU AND THEIR DATE OF BIRTH.

James
(Father)
Born 03.09.1979

Rosie
(Half-sister)
Born 21.07.2012

Amy
(Mother)
Born 05.05.1980

2 START BY PUTTING YOUR OWN NAME IN THE MIDDLE OF THE LARGE PIECE OF PAPER, AT THE BOTTOM, AND THEN ADD ANY ANNOYING BROTHERS AND SISTERS ALONGSIDE IT.

3 IF YOU HAVE HALF- OR STEPBROTHERS AND SISTERS, INCLUDE THEM IN THE ROW(S) ABOVE. COLOUR-CODING HELPS TO MAKE RELATIONSHIPS EASIER TO UNDERSTAND. THE NEXT ROW UP IS FOR YOUR PARENTS AND THE ROW ABOVE THAT IS FOR YOUR GRANDPARENTS.

ME
Born 15.04.2007

Lucas
(Brother)
Born 30.01.2005

Oliver
(Half-brother)
Born 12.10.2013

4 HERE'S ONE EXAMPLE OF A FAMILY TREE. YOURS MIGHT LOOK QUITE DIFFERENT!

GRANDFATHER (FATHER'S SIDE)

GRANDMOTHER (FATHER'S SIDE)

GRANDFATHER (MOTHER'S SIDE)

GRANDMOTHER (MOTHER'S SIDE)

STEPMOTHER

FATHER

MOTHER

STEPFATHER

STEPBROTHER

HALF-SISTER

HALF-BROTHER

STEPSISTER

BROTHER

ME!

SISTER

5 EXTEND YOUR FAMILY TREE BY ADDING AUNTS, UNCLES, COUSINS AND GREAT-GRANDPARENTS. IF YOU RUN OUT OF SPACE, JUST STICK AN EXTRA SHEET OF PAPER TO THE SIDES AND TOP OF THE TREE.

Mary
(Great-aunt)
Born 10.12.1918
Died 13.02.1999

Harry
(Great-grandfather)
Born 03.09.1916
Died 20.08.1991

6 WHEN YOU'RE HAPPY WITH YOUR ROUGH DRAFT, COPY IT NEATLY ONTO A BIGGER PIECE OF PAPER!

TOP TIP:
Ask the oldest person in your family to tell you what pranks and tricks they got up to when they were your age!

HOW TO MAKE
INVISIBLE INK

Send secret messages to your mates that vanish with this brilliant invisible ink recipe!

YOU WILL NEED:

- A LEMON
- WATER
- SMALL PLATE
- TOOTHPICK
- WHITE PAPER
- LAMP

 1 SQUEEZE THE LEMON AND CATCH THE JUICE ON A SMALL PLATE. ADD A FEW DROPS OF WATER AND MIX TOGETHER.

 2 USING THE TOOTHPICK AS A PEN AND THE JUICE AS INK, WRITE YOUR SECRET MESSAGE ON THE PAPER.

 3 WHEN THE INK DRIES, YOUR MESSAGE WILL BE INVISIBLE!

 4 NOW SEND YOUR TOP-SECRET MESSAGE TO ANOTHER MENACE.

 5 HOLD THE PAPER WRITING-SIDE DOWN OVER A LAMP. THE HEAT FROM THE LAMP MAKES THE MESSAGE REAPPEAR, LIKE MAGIC!

I BET YOU CAN SEE RIGHT THROUGH MY PLANS NOW!

BUILD A SECRET
INDOOR DEN

What's better on a rainy day than a super-sized, home-made den? Plus, you can hide inside it while planning all sorts of mischief!

 1 PUT ALL BREAKABLE OBJECTS AWAY. TRY NOT TO USE WEAK OR SMALL PIECES OF FURNITURE THAT MIGHT FALL DOWN ON THE PEOPLE INSIDE THE DEN.

 2 DRAPE BLANKETS, SHEETS AND TOWELS OVER LARGE PIECES OF FURNITURE LIKE A DINING TABLE, THE BACK OF AN ARMCHAIR OR SOFA.

 3 USE CHAIRS TO PROP UP YOUR SHEETS, TOO. TURN THEM AROUND SO THEY CAN BE USED AS TABLES INSIDE THE DEN.

 4 SHEETS MAKE THE BEST ROOFS BECAUSE THEY'RE LIGHT. KEEP THEM IN PLACE WITH BULLDOG CLIPS OR CUSHIONS.

 5 FILL YOUR DEN WITH FUN THINGS TO DO. BOOKS, GAMES AND SNACKS ARE PERFECT!

 6 THE INSIDE OF YOUR DEN SHOULD BE COMFY AND COSY. FILL THE FLOOR WITH CUSHIONS, SO YOU'VE ALWAYS GOT SOMEWHERE SQUISHY TO SIT. FINISHED!

GROW CRAZY BEANO
CRESS HEADS

Show the world just how creative you can be by making these totally eggy works of art!

YOU WILL NEED:

- CRESS SEEDS
- TWO BOILED OR RAW EGGS
- EGGCUPS OR EGG BOXES
- KITCHEN TOWEL
- COTTON WOOL
- FELT TIPS OR PAINT
- GOOGLY EYES (OPTIONAL)

1 IF YOU'RE USING BOILED EGGS, EAT THE EGGS FIRST – THEY'RE DELICIOUS WITH TOAST SOLDIERS! OTHERWISE, ASK AN ADULT TO BREAK THE TOP OFF THE EGGS AND EMPTY THEM OUT INTO A BOWL.

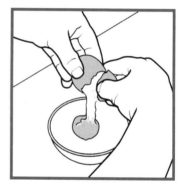

2

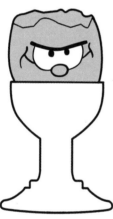

CAREFULLY CLEAN OUT THE INSIDES OF THE EGGSHELLS, THEN PUT THE EGGS IN EGGCUPS OR EGG BOXES.

3 WET A PIECE OF KITCHEN TOWEL AND SCREW IT UP INSIDE THE SHELL. THEN, WET A PIECE OF COTTON WOOL AND PUT IT ON TOP.

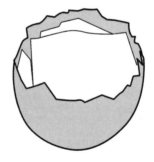

THESE CRAZY CRESS HEADS ARE EGGS-ELLENT!

4 SPRINKLE A LAYER OF CRESS SEEDS ON THE COTTON WOOL AND PUT THE EGGS ON A SUNNY WINDOWSILL. KEEP THE COTTON WOOL MOIST BUT NOT WET.

 5 IN ABOUT A WEEK, THE CRESS SHOULD BE ABOUT 4 CM TALL. NOW, YOU CAN SNIP IT OFF AND EAT IT ON ITS OWN OR IN A TASTY SANDWICH!

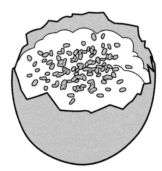

 6 HERE COMES THE REALLY FUN PART. GRAB YOUR FELT TIPS OR PAINTS AND DECORATE THE EGGS. TRY DRAWING YOUR FAVOURITE BEANO CHARACTER'S FACE ON EACH ONE!

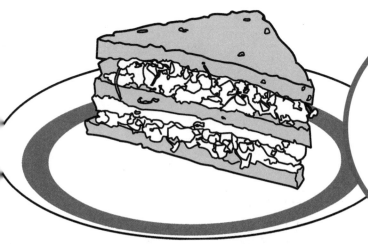

TOP TIP:
Make a mini greenhouse from a plastic bottle with the top cut off and put it over one eggshell. It should make the cress grow faster!

31

MIND-BLOWING
CARD TRICKS

Here's your chance to wow your friends and family – all you need is a normal pack of playing cards!

COLOUR CARD TRICK

 1 SEPARATE THE CARDS INTO BLACK AND RED PILES. REMEMBER WHICH COLOUR CARD YOU PLACED ON TOP OF EACH PILE. DO THIS BEFORE YOU START YOUR PERFORMANCE, SO THAT YOUR AUDIENCE DOESN'T SEE!

 2 FAN OUT THE TOP FEW CARDS, WITH THE BACKS FACING YOUR AUDIENCE, AND ASK A VOLUNTEER TO PICK A CARD FROM THE TOP. TELL THEM TO MEMORISE THE CARD THEY CHOSE.

 3 FAN OUT THE BOTTOM OF THE DECK AND THEN ASK THEM TO REPLACE THEIR CARD. NO PEEKING!

 4 SPLIT THE DECK SOMEWHERE IN THE MIDDLE, AND PLACE THE BOTTOM HALF ON THE TOP TO "SHUFFLE" THE CARDS. IT DOESN'T MATTER IF THE SPLIT ISN'T EXACTLY IN THE MIDDLE.

5 TO MAGICALLY FIND THE CARD THAT WAS CHOSEN, LOOK THROUGH THE DECK. THE COLOUR OF THE ONE YOU WANT SHOULD BE THE ONLY RED CARD MIXED IN BETWEEN THE BLACK CARDS OR VICE VERSA.

6 PULL OUT THE CARD AND ANNOUNCE, "IS THIS YOUR CARD?" YOUR AUDIENCE WILL BE AMAZED WITH YOUR TOTALLY BRILLIANT MIND-READING MAGIC SKILLS!

FIND THE CARD

1 BEFORE YOU PERFORM THIS TRICK, CHECK WHICH CARD IS AT THE BOTTOM OF THE PACK.

2 ASK A MEMBER OF YOUR AUDIENCE TO SELECT A CARD.

3 SPLIT THE DECK AND ASK THEM TO RETURN THEIR CARD TO THE TOP PART OF THE DECK.

4 PLACE THE BOTTOM PART ON TOP, SO THAT THE CARD YOU KNOW THE NUMBER OF IS NOW SITTING NEXT TO THE CHOSEN CARD.

WAIT, WHAT?! THAT'S AMAZING!

5 ASK THE AUDIENCE MEMBER TO CUT THE PACK A COUPLE MORE TIMES.

6 LIFT THE CARDS WITH THE FACES TOWARDS YOU AND LOOK FOR YOUR MEMORISED CARD. THE CARD UNDERNEATH IT IS THE AUDIENCE MEMBER'S CARD. IT'S JUST LIKE MAGIC!

TOTALLY AWESOME
MAGIC TRICKS

Have you ever wanted to become a master magician?
Try these tricks at school to impress your mates!

PRETEND TO MAKE YOUR HEAD FALL OFF!

YOU WILL NEED:
- A BUTTON-UP JACKET
- TWO UMBRELLAS WITH HOOKED ENDS

1 MAKE A CROSS WITH THE UMBRELLAS BENEATH YOUR CHIN AND PLACE THEM ON YOUR SHOULDERS UNDER THE JACKET. ONE HAND SHOULD BE IN YOUR POCKET, SO THAT YOU CAN MOVE THEM WHEN NEEDED.

2 PRETEND TO SNEEZE, DROPPING YOUR HEAD DOWN TOWARDS YOUR HAND. AT THE SAME TIME, PUSH THE UMBRELLAS UP, SO IT LOOKS LIKE YOUR SHOULDERS HAVEN'T MOVED BUT YOUR HEAD HAS SUDDENLY FALLEN OFF!

3 WATCH AS YOUR AUDIENCE IS WOWED BY YOUR MAGICAL FLOATING HEAD! PUSH YOUR HEAD BACK UP AND PULL THE UMBRELLAS BACK DOWN – IT WILL LOOK LIKE YOU'VE MAGICALLY PUT YOUR HEAD BACK ON. IT'S SUCH A COOL TRICK!

LEARN THIS TRICK TO GET A-HEAD OF THE GAME!

PRETEND TO FLY!

YOU WILL NEED:
- A JUG OF WATER

1 YOU'LL NEED TO DO THIS TRICK SOMEWHERE OUTSIDE! POUR WATER ONTO THE GROUND, TO CREATE A SMALL CIRCLE THAT WILL BE YOUR PRETEND SHADOW.

2 NOW MOVE ONE STEP BACKWARDS AND TWO STEPS TO THE RIGHT.

3 GET SOMEONE TO TAKE YOUR PHOTO. THE WET PATCH WILL LOOK LIKE YOUR SHADOW AND YOU'LL SEEM TO BE FLYING. ABRACADABRA!

WORM JUICE

YUM! DID SOMEONE SAY FLY?

SUPERHERO TRAINING

ARE YOU UP FOR THE CHALLENGE, CHUMS?

Do you have what it takes to become a real hero? Find out with Bananaman's superhuman tests!

CHALLENGE 1:

Blow up two balloons and throw them into the air together. Keep them in the air for 60 seconds. If they hit the ground – you're out!

CHALLENGE 2:

This one is harder than it looks! Attach an empty tissue box to your bottom using string. Fill it with seven ping-pong balls. Now you have 60 seconds to shake them all out!

CHALLENGE 3:

Place twelve plastic cups around the floor in a circle. Put a tennis ball inside each foot of a pair of tights. Put the tights on your head, so the tennis balls are dangling. Now, swing away and try to knock all the cups over in under a minute!

CHALLENGE 4:

Hold a lollipop stick in your mouth with most of it sticking out. Get someone else to balance twelve sugar cubes on the end of it. You have to hold them there for at least three seconds without dropping any!

CHALLENGE 5:

Move a cookie from your forehead to your mouth without using your hands! Sit on a chair, tip your head back and place the cookie on your forehead, not touching your eyebrows. Use the muscles in your face to move it to your mouth. If it drops, replace with another cookie and try again!

CHALLENGE 6:

Prove you're a real fruit ninja by flicking playing cards at a halved watermelon and see if you can get one to stick in it!

CHALLENGE 7:

You need unsharpened pencils – the kind with rubbers on the end – for this challenge. You have to get them to bounce on their rubber end and flip into a cup. Get one pencil into the cup in under 60 seconds to pass!

CHALLENGE 8:

Hang up a toilet roll, with a long strip dangling down to the ground. Weigh down the strip by tying an empty can to the bottom of the toilet paper. Now sit 8 feet away at a table. Shoot rubber bands at the toilet paper and get it to break in under 60 seconds!

TASTEBUD TRIATHLON

Get your tastebuds tingling with this freaky mystery-blindfold taste test!

YOU WILL NEED:
- A BLINDFOLD
- PLASTIC SPOONS
- A SELECTION OF FOOD, SUCH AS MAYONNAISE, MASHED BANANA, CHEESE, CHOCOLATE, CUCUMBER, KETCHUP, APPLE, KIWI FRUIT, STRAWBERRIES, JAM OR HONEY

1 KEEP ALL THE FOODS HIDDEN AND BLINDFOLD ONE OR MORE PLAYERS.

2 PUT A LITTLE BIT OF ONE FOOD ON A SPOON AND ASK THE BLINDFOLDED PLAYER(S) TO TASTE IT AND GUESS WHAT IT IS. NO PEEKING!

3 PLAYERS GET A POINT FOR EACH FOOD THEY GUESS CORRECTLY!

TOP TIP:
If you have lots of players you could play in two teams, with one team preparing foods for the other!

SAFETY FIRST!
Make sure that all the foods are safe to eat and don't give anyone raw meat or fish. Ask an adult to cut up the fruit and vegetables, washing them before eating!

EDIBLE SNOT

Totally gross **EVERYONE** out and make sticky, gooey, tasty bogies. YUM, YUM!

YOU WILL NEED:
- CAN OF SWEETENED CONDENSED MILK
- 2 TABLESPOONS OF CORNFLOUR
- GREEN FOOD COLOURING

1 POUR THE CAN OF CONDENSED MILK INTO A SAUCEPAN.

2 ADD 2 TABLESPOONS OF CORNFLOUR TO THE MILK AND MIX TOGETHER.

3 ASK AN ADULT TO HELP YOU WARM THE MIXTURE OVER A LOW HEAT FOR A FEW MINUTES.

4 POUR THE MIXTURE INTO A BOWL AND ALLOW IT TO COOL.

5 MIX IN A FEW DROPS OF GREEN FOOD COLOURING.

6 NOW GET YOUR HANDS COVERED IN SNOT AND TUCK IN. GROSS!

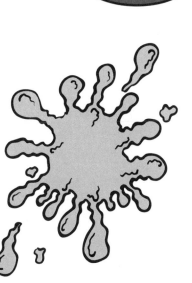

MMM... YUMMY. BOGIES!

ER... I'M GOING TO BE SICK!

BLAST OFF A
BALLOON ROCKET

Your mum and dad might think you're full of hot air - so time to put it to good use!

YOU WILL NEED:
- BALLOONS
- PLASTIC STRAW
- STICKY TAPE
- STRING

1 TIE ONE END OF THE STRING TO A DOORKNOB OR THE BACK OF A CHAIR – ANY OBJECT THAT'S AROUND THAT HEIGHT.

2 THREAD THE OTHER END OF THE STRING THROUGH A STRAW.

TRY HAVING A ROCKET RACE WITH YOUR MATES!

MY PRANKS
WON'T STOP TILL
THIS BALLOON
GOES POP!

 PULL THE STRING TIGHT AND TIE THE
OTHER END TO SOMETHING ELSE IN
THE ROOM AT THE SAME HEIGHT.

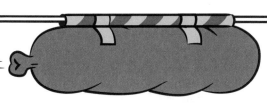

 BLOW UP THE BALLOON, PINCH THE
END SO THAT THE AIR DOESN'T
ESCAPE AND GET SOMEONE TO HELP
TAPE THE BALLOON TO THE STRAW.

5 PULL THE BALLOON ALONG TO THE
END OF THE STRING, LET IT GO AND
YOUR ROCKET WILL FLY. WHOOSH!

DID YOU KNOW?

The heat produced
by a rocket's thrusters
at lift-off could heat
85,000 homes
for a day!

MAKE A MINI PAPER CLIP
SLINGSHOT

A true Menace can make a MEGA weapon out of just about anything!

YOU WILL NEED:
- A LARGE PAPER CLIP
- A RUBBER BAND
- PAPER
- A HELPFUL ADULT

 ASK AN ADULT TO DO ALL OF THE MUSCLE WORK!
THEY'LL NEED TO STRAIGHTEN OUT THE PAPER CLIP.

 GET THEM TO BEND THE PAPER
CLIP INTO A U-SHAPE LIKE THIS:

THESE EMPTY YOGHURT POTS MAKE GREAT TARGETS, GNASHER!

WHOOSH!

3 ON EACH SIDE OF THE U-SHAPE, BEND THE TOP TO MAKE A CURVE AT THE SIDES FOR THE RUBBER BAND TO ATTACH TO. CUT THE BAND IN HALF AND TIE ONE END EITHER SIDE OF THE U-SHAPE. ONE MINI PAPER CLIP SLINGSHOT COMPLETE!

4 FOLD SMALL SCRAPS OF PAPER UP INTO V-SHAPES FOR AMMUNITION. NOW FIND A TARGET TO AIM AT AND... KA-POW!

SAFETY FIRST!
Make sure you never aim your paper clip slingshot at animals or people!

TREASURE HUNT

This is a fantastic treasure hunt to play with your fellow Menaces!

YOU WILL NEED:
- 8-10 LOLLY OR CRAFT STICKS
- STICKY TAPE
- MARKER PENS
- TREASURE, SUCH AS SWEETS, CAKES OR A SMALL TOY

1 STICK THE LOLLY OR CRAFT STICKS TOGETHER WITH STICKY TAPE AND THEN WRITE DOWN CLUES TO FIND THE TREASURE BY WRITING ONE LETTER ON EACH STICK.

2 TURN THE STICKS OVER AND DRAW A PICTURE ON THE FRONT. THEN TAKE THE TAPE OFF THE STICKS SO THEY'RE SEPARATE AND SNEAKILY HIDE THEM ALL IN ONE ROOM!

3 TO DISCOVER WHERE THE TREASURE IS HIDDEN, EVERYONE NEEDS TO FIND ALL OF THE STICKS AND ARRANGE THEM IN THE CORRECT ORDER, USING THE PICTURE ON THE FRONT AS A GUIDE. GO FOR IT!

YUM! I GET TO EAT ALL THE BOOTY!

SUPER STICKY
SPIDERWEB

I use this cool web trap to stop my mum and dad barging into my room!

YOU WILL NEED:
- MASKING TAPE OR STICKY TAPE
- BALLS OF CRUMPLED NEWSPAPER

 THIS IS SO EASY TO DO! JUST STICK MASKING TAPE OR STICKY TAPE ACROSS AN OPEN DOORWAY TO FORM A WEB PATTERN, WITH THE STICKY SIDE FACING YOU.

 THE BALLS OF NEWSPAPER ARE YOUR FLIES. TRY TO THROW THEM THROUGH THE GAPS IN THE WEB WITHOUT THEM GETTING CAUGHT. IF MOST OF YOUR FLIES MAKE IT THROUGH TO THE OTHER SIDE, TRY ADDING MORE TAPE TO MAKE SOME OF THE GAPS SMALLER AND TRICKIER!

TOP TIP:
You could also take it in turns standing in front of the web like a giant spider, trying to block everyone else's shot!

RUBBER BAND
BAZOOKA BLASTER

Transform your boring old pencils into an explosive Rubber Band Bazooka Blaster! Take that, homework! POW!

YOU WILL NEED:
- 3 PENCILS WITH RUBBERS ON THE END
- LOTS OF RUBBER BANDS

I'M HAVING A BLAST!

1 FIRST, MAKE A CROSS SHAPE WITH TWO PENCILS.

2 PLACE ANOTHER PENCIL ON TOP AND HOLD THEM ALL TOGETHER BY TYING THE TOP PENCIL TO THE BOTTOM PENCIL WITH RUBBER BANDS. THE MIDDLE ONE SHOULD BE HELD BETWEEN THEM. THE RUBBER BAND CLOSEST TO THE SHARP END OF THE PENCIL SHOULD BE SLIGHTLY LOOSER THAN THE BACK ELASTIC BAND SO IT CAN MOVE.

3 LOAD YOUR BAZOOKA BLASTER BY LOOPING AN ELASTIC BAND ONTO THE RUBBER AT THE BOTTOM OF THE BAZOOKA. STRETCH IT BACK AND TUCK IT UNDER THE TRIGGER (THE OTHER RUBBER). DONE!

4 NOW YOU'RE READY FOR ACTION! TAKE AIM, PUSH DOWN ON THE TOP PENCIL TO RELEASE THE TRIGGER AND... FIRE!

KAPOW! HERE I COME!

SAFETY FIRST!
Never aim your bazooka blaster at animals or people!

47

HOUSE OF CARDS

Bamboozle your friends with this totally amazing card-stacking trick!

YOU WILL NEED:

- PLAYING CARDS
- A FLAT SURFACE AND A STEADY HAND!

 1 BALANCE TWO CARDS AGAINST EACH OTHER TO MAKE A TRIANGLE SHAPE AND CONTINUE UNTIL YOU HAVE A LINE OF THREE TRIANGLES.

2 CAREFULLY LAY TWO CARDS ON TOP, THEN ADD TWO MORE TRIANGLE SHAPES.

3 LAY ONE CARD ON TOP OF THOSE SHAPES AND THEN MAKE A TRIANGLE WITH TWO CARDS ON TOP OF THAT TO MAKE THE THIRD STOREY. EASY!

TOP TIP:
Challenge a friend to see who can build the tallest house first!

OOOH! A NEW DOG HOUSE!

MARBLE RUN

See if you can become a marble speed champion with this awesome indoor racing game!

YOU WILL NEED:

- CARDBOARD TUBES AND PLASTIC BOTTLES
- A TALL CARDBOARD BOX WITH THE TOP AND FRONT CUT OFF (OPTIONAL)
- MASKING TAPE
- MARBLES
- A CONTAINER TO CATCH THE MARBLES (E.G. THE BOTTOM OF A PLASTIC BOTTLE)

1 ASK AN ADULT TO CUT THE CARDBOARD TUBES IN HALF LENGTHWAYS. THEN ASK THEM TO CUT THE BOTTLES IN HALF ACROSS THE MIDDLE.

2 STARTING AT THE TOP, TAPE THE TUBES AND BOTTLES TO THE BACK OF THE BOX. MAKE SURE THEY SLOPE DOWNWARDS AND THAT WHEN A MARBLE DROPS, THERE'S A TUBE OR BOTTLE BELOW TO CATCH IT.

3 PLACE A CONTAINER AT THE END OF THE RUN AT THE BOTTOM TO CATCH THE MARBLES, THEN LET THEM LOOSE!

COME ON, MARBLES, LET'S RACE!

TOP TIP:

If you don't have any marbles, use balls of rolled-up aluminium foil!

KIDS-ONLY

INDOOR TEEPEE

Who cares about the rubbish weather outside when you can go camping indoors?

WHAT IF YOU NEED A TEE-PEE?

YOU WILL NEED:
- 6 TALL BAMBOO CANES
- STRING
- BLANKETS OR SHEETS
- 12 CLOTHES PEGS
- CUSHIONS, RUGS AND PILLOWS

1 FIRST, TIE THE CANES TOGETHER WITH STRING, ABOUT 20 CM FROM THE TOP.

2 REST THE BOTTOMS OF THE CANES ON THE FLOOR AND PULL THEM OUT TO MAKE A TEEPEE SHAPE. THIS IS EASIER IF YOU HAVE SOMEONE TO HELP YOU!

WORM YOGHURT

TOP TIP:
Arrange some pillows around the outside of your teepee to keep the canes in place!

3 DRAPE BLANKETS OR SHEETS AROUND THE CANES AND PEG THEM IN PLACE AT THE TOP AND BOTTOM, THEN FILL YOUR TEEPEE WITH PILLOWS, RUGS AND CUSHIONS. FINISHED!

DID YOU KNOW?
Teepees were built by Native Americans and some could hold up to 30–40 people!

I'M SLEEPING IN HERE ALL NIGHT!

ER... WHAT WAS THE PASSWORD AGAIN?

TOP-SECRET BASE!

KIDS ONLY!

SMIFFY'S SMIRKERS

When you're bored indoors, freak out your parents with these gross gags!

How do you keep an elephant from charging? **Take away its credit card!**

What do you call a goat dressed as a clown? **A silly billy!**

What do you call an alligator in a vest? **An investi-gator!**

How do you stop a dog barking in the back of your car? **Put him in the front!**

What do you call a pig that knows karate? **A pork chop!**

Why do fish live in salt water? **Because pepper makes them sneeze!**

What fish tastes best with ice cream? **A jelly-fish!**

What do you get from nervous cows? **Milkshakes!**

Who is the king of the classroom? **The ruler!**

Why did the man sit under a cow? He wanted a pat on the head!

What do you call it when criminals go surfing? **A crime wave!**

What do you call a green fly with no legs or wings? **A bogey!**

What kind of dance do plumbers like? **Tap-dancing!**

Can February march? **No, but April May!**

Why do singers never lock themselves out? **They always find the right key!**

Where do sheep go on holiday? **The Baaaaahamas!**

What do you get if you cross a footballer with a ghost? **A ghoulie!**

Who works on a ghost ship? **A skeleton crew!**

Knock, knock. Who's there? Spell. Spell who? W-H-O!

What does a thunder god say when he's hurt? **"I'm Thor!"**

53

CREATIVE FUN!

It's time to get creative with all sorts of totally awesome activities. These fun ideas will really impress your mates AND get you into all sorts of mischief. Gnash!

MAKE A SUPER SPY
PERISCOPE

Check that the coast is clear after a cheeky prank with this brilliant periscope!

YOU WILL NEED:
- 2 TALL JUICE OR MILK CARTONS
- A CRAFT KNIFE
- A RULER
- PENCIL OR PEN
- 2 SMALL FLAT MIRRORS
- MASKING TAPE

1 ASK AN ADULT TO CUT THE TOPS OFF BOTH CARTONS. CUT A SMALL WINDOW AT THE BOTTOM OF EACH CARTON, LEAVING ABOUT 7 MM AROUND THE SIDES OF THE HOLE. THEN WASH THEM OUT.

2 STARTING AT ONE CORNER, ASK AN ADULT TO MAKE A CUT THE LENGTH OF ONE SIDE OF YOUR MIRROR ALONG THE DIAGONAL LINE.

3 PUT ONE CARTON ON ITS SIDE, WITH THE HOLE FACING TO YOUR RIGHT. MEASURE THE BOTTOM OF THE CARTON, THEN MEASURE THE SAME DISTANCE ON THE LEFT–HAND SIDE OF THE CARTON AND MAKE A MARK. DRAW A DIAGONAL LINE BETWEEN THE MARK AND THE BOTTOM–RIGHT CORNER.

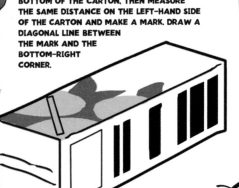

SAFETY FIRST!
Ask an adult to help you cut the carton!

NOW I'LL BE ABLE TO SEE ALL THE BEST PLACES TO PRANK!

4 SLIDE THE MIRROR INTO THE SLOT, SO YOU CAN SEE IT THROUGH THE HOLE IN THE FRONT. YOU SHOULD BE ABLE TO SEE THE CEILING THROUGH THE TOP OF THE CARTON. WHEN IT'S IN THE RIGHT POSITION, TAPE IT SECURELY IN PLACE. REPEAT STEPS 2–4 WITH THE OTHER CARTON.

 5 STAND ONE CARTON THE RIGHT WAY UP WITH THE HOLE FACING YOU, THEN PLACE THE OTHER CARTON UPSIDE DOWN ON TOP, WITH THE HOLE FACING AWAY FROM YOU.

 6 SQUEEZE THE BOTTOM OF THE UPSIDE-DOWN CARTON, SO IT SLIDES A LITTLE WAY INSIDE THE BOTTOM CARTON, THEN TAPE THE TWO TOGETHER.

TOP TIP:
If you turn your periscope upside down, you can look under tables or into the bottom bunk of a bed, too!

ER... IT FEELS LIKE SOMEONE'S WATCHING ME!

HOW TO BECOME A
CATAPULT CHAMPION

The ULTIMATE Menace weapon! You'll get into all sorts of trouble with this essential bit of mischief-making kit!

YOU WILL NEED:

- 6 PENCILS
- RUBBER BANDS
- PLASTIC SPOON
- SOFT PROJECTILES (E.G. FOAM OR PAPER BALLS)

1 USING THE RUBBER BANDS, TIE THREE OF THE PENCILS TOGETHER, THEN USE THE REMAINING PENCILS TO FORM A SQUARE FRAME.

2 NOW, WITH MORE RUBBER BANDS, ATTACH THE SPOON TO THE THREE PENCILS AT THE FRONT OF THE FRAME.

THE FURTHER BACK THAT YOU PULL THE SPOON, THE LONGER YOUR CATAPULT SHOT WILL BE!

3 NOW, YOU'RE READY TO LAUNCH YOUR CATAPULT – LOAD THE PROJECTILE INTO THE SPOON, PULL IT BACK, AIM AND FIRE!

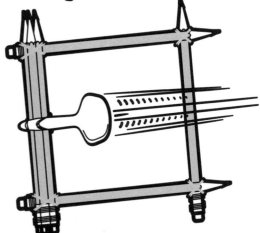

CRAZY CATAPULT GAMES TO PLAY ON YOUR OWN!

GAME 1: BUCKET SHOT
Set up a bucket or pot and try to land your projectile inside!

GAME 2: ULTIMATE ACCURACY
Stand a few coloured pencils on their ends in a cup. Can you knock the red one over without hitting any of the others?

GAME 3: CHAIN REACTION
Place a few toys in a line, then fire at one so that it knocks all the others over!

TAKE ON A FRIEND IN THESE COOL CATAPULT CHALLENGES!

GAME 1: LONG SHOT
See who can fire their projectile the furthest!

GAME 2: BLINDFOLD CHALLENGE
Set up some targets, then see who can hit the most ... while wearing a blindfold!

GAME 3: QUICK SHOT
See who can launch the most projectiles the fastest!

NOW TO TEST OUT MY CATAPULT ON WALTER'S NICE CLEAN SHOES!

WHAT DENNIS USES HIS CATAPULT FOR:
Dennis' favourite things to launch from his catapult are tomatoes!

They fly really well and make a great SPLAT when they hit their target!

FORTUNE-TELLER

Hee hee! I'm going to write some really yucky messages in MY fortune-teller!

YOU WILL NEED:

- A PIECE OF PAPER
- SCISSORS
- COLOURED PENCILS OR MARKERS

1 START BY FOLDING THE PAPER DIAGONALLY AND CUT OFF THE RECTANGLE AT THE TOP TO LEAVE A PERFECT SQUARE. FOLD IT AGAIN TO MAKE A SMALLER TRIANGLE. THIS WILL GIVE YOU THE CENTRE POINT.

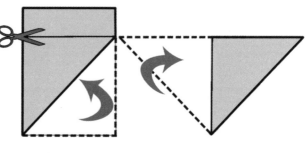

2 OPEN OUT THE PAPER AND FOLD THE FOUR CORNERS INTO THE CENTRE.

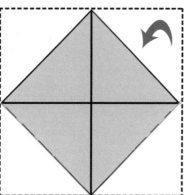

3 TURN THE SQUARE OVER AND FOLD THE FOUR CORNERS INTO THE CENTRE AGAIN. WRITE THE NUMBERS ONE TO EIGHT ON EACH OF THE SMALL TRIANGLES. HALFWAY THERE!

I CAN TELL YOU MY FUTURE. I'M OFF TO CAUSE MAYHEM!

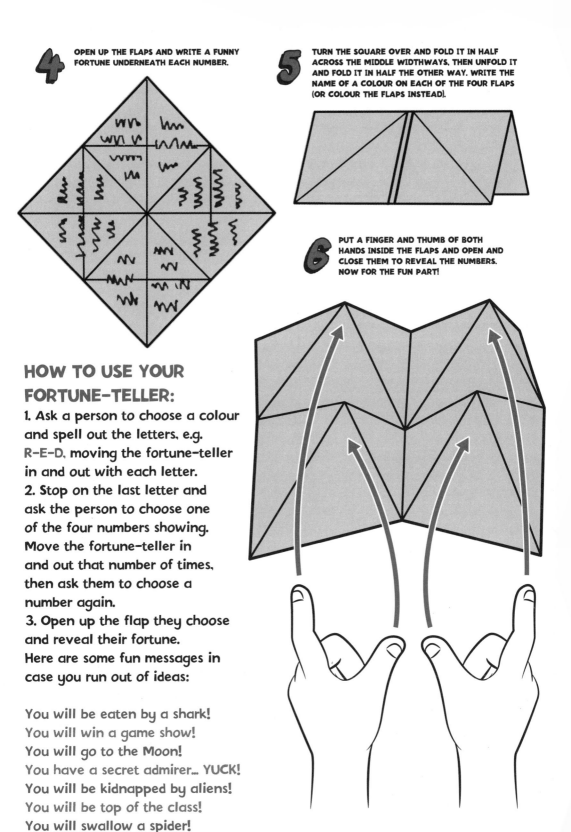

4 OPEN UP THE FLAPS AND WRITE A FUNNY FORTUNE UNDERNEATH EACH NUMBER.

5 TURN THE SQUARE OVER AND FOLD IT IN HALF ACROSS THE MIDDLE WIDTHWAYS, THEN UNFOLD IT AND FOLD IT IN HALF THE OTHER WAY. WRITE THE NAME OF A COLOUR ON EACH OF THE FOUR FLAPS (OR COLOUR THE FLAPS INSTEAD).

6 PUT A FINGER AND THUMB OF BOTH HANDS INSIDE THE FLAPS AND OPEN AND CLOSE THEM TO REVEAL THE NUMBERS. NOW FOR THE FUN PART!

HOW TO USE YOUR FORTUNE-TELLER:

1. Ask a person to choose a colour and spell out the letters, e.g. R-E-D, moving the fortune-teller in and out with each letter.
2. Stop on the last letter and ask the person to choose one of the four numbers showing. Move the fortune-teller in and out that number of times, then ask them to choose a number again.
3. Open up the flap they choose and reveal their fortune.
Here are some fun messages in case you run out of ideas:

You will be eaten by a shark!
You will win a game show!
You will go to the Moon!
You have a secret admirer... YUCK!
You will be kidnapped by aliens!
You will be top of the class!
You will swallow a spider!

ULTIMATE PAPER
PIRATE SHIP

You'll be the scourge of the Seven Seas with these awesome paper vessels!

YOU WILL NEED:

- SHEETS OF PAPER
- WAX CRAYONS (OPTIONAL)
- COCKTAIL STICKS, MARKERS OR PAINTS (OPTIONAL)
- A BATH

1 START BY FOLDING THE PAPER IN HALF ACROSS THE MIDDLE AND FOLD THE TOP CORNERS IN, SO THEY MEET IN THE CENTRE.

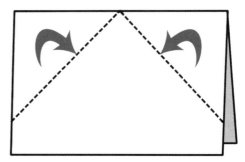

2 FOLD THE TOP OF THE OBLONG FLAP AT THE BOTTOM UP OVER THE TRIANGLE ABOVE, THEN TURN THE PAPER OVER AND DO THE SAME ON THE OTHER SIDE.

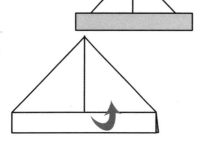

3 OPEN UP THE TRIANGLE SHAPE (JUST LIKE A HAT!) AND PUSH THE SIDES TOGETHER TO FORM A SQUARE.

I'M THIRSTY. DID SOMEONE SAY THERE'S A SALE ON WATER?

4 FOLD THE TWO BOTTOM CORNERS UP TO THE TOP TO FORM A TRIANGLE, THEN PUSH THE TWO SIDES TOGETHER AGAIN TO FORM A SQUARE.

5 PULL THE SIDE FLAPS APART AND A BOAT SHAPE WILL APPEAR. PUT YOUR FINGERS INSIDE THE TRIANGLE IN THE CENTRE AND GENTLY PULL IT APART SO YOUR PIRATE SHIP STANDS UP.

6 DECORATE YOUR SHIPS, THEN PUT A SMALL AMOUNT OF COLD WATER IN THE BATH AND SEE HOW WELL THEY FLOAT. TRY CREATING A BREEZE BY FLAPPING A NEWSPAPER AT ONE END OF THE BATH TO SPEED THEM ALONG!

TOP TIP: If you colour the outside of your boat with wax crayons, it will last longer in the water!

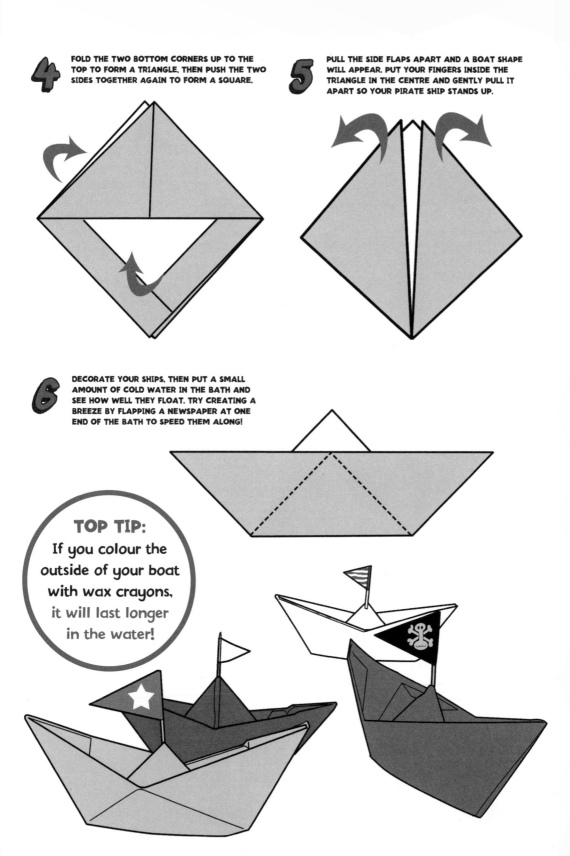

AQUA ATTACK!

Parents snooping in your bedroom all the time?
Scare them away with these toothy creatures!

YOU WILL NEED:

- 6 SMALL WHITE PAPER PLATES
- 2 LARGE WHITE PAPER PLATES
- PAINTS
- PAINTBRUSH
- 6 GOOGLY EYES
- GLUE
- SCISSORS

1 TO MAKE THE PIRANHA FISH, PAINT THE BACKS OF FOUR OF THE SMALL PAPER PLATES IN BRIGHT COLOURS.

2 WHILE THEY'RE DRYING, CUT FINS AND TAILS FROM THE OTHER TWO SMALL PLATES AND PAINT THEM.

3 GLUE THE FINS AND TAILS TO THE OTHER SIDES OF THE SMALL PAINTED PLATES, AND DECORATE THE FISH WITH SHARP TEETH, STRIPES AND OTHER PATTERNS. GLUE ON THE GOOGLY EYES AND ARRANGE THE FISH ON YOUR WALL!

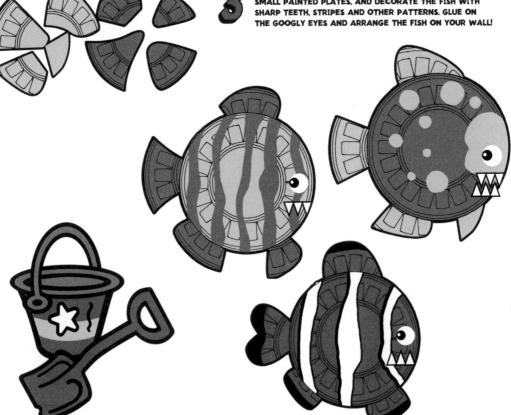

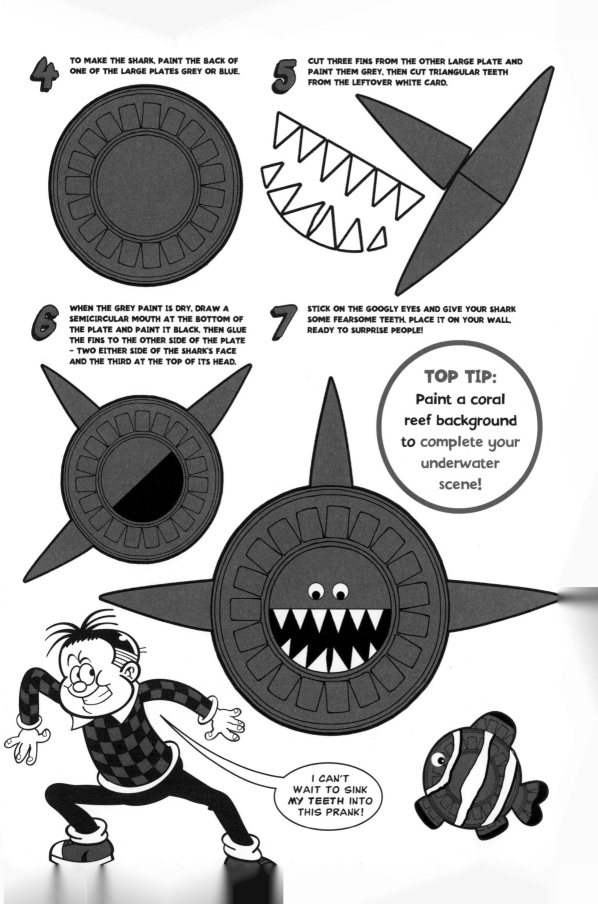

4 TO MAKE THE SHARK, PAINT THE BACK OF ONE OF THE LARGE PLATES GREY OR BLUE.

5 CUT THREE FINS FROM THE OTHER LARGE PLATE AND PAINT THEM GREY, THEN CUT TRIANGULAR TEETH FROM THE LEFTOVER WHITE CARD.

6 WHEN THE GREY PAINT IS DRY, DRAW A SEMICIRCULAR MOUTH AT THE BOTTOM OF THE PLATE AND PAINT IT BLACK. THEN GLUE THE FINS TO THE OTHER SIDE OF THE PLATE – TWO EITHER SIDE OF THE SHARK'S FACE AND THE THIRD AT THE TOP OF ITS HEAD.

7 STICK ON THE GOOGLY EYES AND GIVE YOUR SHARK SOME FEARSOME TEETH. PLACE IT ON YOUR WALL, READY TO SURPRISE PEOPLE!

TOP TIP: Paint a coral reef background to complete your underwater scene!

I CAN'T WAIT TO SINK MY TEETH INTO THIS PRANK!

SOCK PUPPET
SIDEKICK

Create a sock puppet to make all sorts of mischief. If you get caught out, just blame it on the puppet!

YOU WILL NEED:

- LARGE SOCK
- PIECE OF THICK CARDBOARD
- SCISSORS
- WOOL (OPTIONAL)
- 2 BUTTONS, GOOGLY EYES, PIPE CLEANERS AND OTHER CRAFT BITS YOU CAN FIND
- FABRIC GLUE

1 CUT A LARGE OVAL SHAPE FROM THE CARDBOARD AND FOLD IT IN HALF. THIS WILL BE YOUR PUPPET'S BIG MOUTH!

2 DECORATE THE OVAL SO IT LOOKS LIKE A MOUTH. YOU COULD ADD A TONGUE, TEETH OR EVEN WORDS!

3 STICK YOUR HAND INSIDE THE SOCK AND FIND THE "MOUTH". PUT YOUR THUMB IN THE HEEL OF THE SOCK AND YOUR OTHER FINGERS IN THE TOES.

4 DOT SOME FABRIC GLUE INSIDE THE CREASE AND INSERT THE CARDBOARD MOUTH. LEAVE IT TO DRY.

WELL DONE. WHAT AN AMAZING "FEET"!

5 DECORATE YOUR PUPPET WITH OTHER MATERIALS TO MAKE IT MORE LIKE AN ORIGINAL CHARACTER: A FAKE WIG (USING WOOL), FUNNY EARS (WITH PIPE CLEANERS) OR EVEN A COOL SUPERHERO CAPE!

Now you've created your amazing puppet, it's time to make it talk!

 1 CAPTURE YOUR AUDIENCE'S ATTENTION BY SAYING SOMETHING AS SIMPLE AS, "DID YOU HEAR THAT?" THE QUESTION WILL MAKE THEM LISTEN MORE CLOSELY.

 2 TRY TO "SWALLOW" YOUR ACTUAL VOICE AND SPEAK, MOVING YOUR MOUTH AS LITTLE AS POSSIBLE. YOU WANT TO CONTROL YOUR BREATHING AND TALK FROM "INSIDE" YOUR MOUTH.

 3 SAYING THE LETTERS B, F, M, P, Q, V AND W IS VERY CHALLENGING. TRY USING THE SUBSTITUTIONS IN THE CHART BELOW.

B Replace it with a "geh" sound at the back of the throat

F Use a "th" sound, so "fabulous" becomes "thabulous"

M Use "nah" or "neh" instead, so "master" becomes "nah-ster"

P Use "kl" in the back of your throat, so "paint" becomes "klaint"

Q Stretch out the sound so it's "koo"

V Just like F, use the "th" sound

W Use "oooh" at the start of a word, so "welcome" would sound like "oooh-elcome"

LAVA LAMP

The cool blobs you see in a lava lamp are easy to create – you can even make them glow!

YOU WILL NEED:
- CLEAN PLASTIC BOTTLE WITH CAP (1.5 L)
- COOKING OIL
- WATER
- FOOD COLOURING
- ROCK SALT
- TORCH

1 FILL ¼ OF THE BOTTLE WITH WATER AND THE REMAINING ¾ WITH OIL. ADD ABOUT 10 DROPS OF FOOD COLOURING.

2 DROP IN THE ROCK SALT AND SCREW ON THE CAP. NOW WATCH THE COLOURED BUBBLES RISE AS THE SALT FIZZES!

3 TURN OUT THE LIGHTS AND SHINE A TORCH UNDER THE BOTTOM OF THE BOTTLE. YOU MADE THAT COOL SPECIAL EFFECT. WAY TO GO!

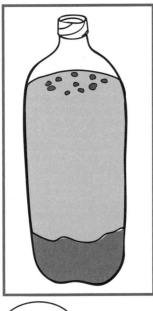

WOW! THAT'S A PRETTY BLOB!

HOW TO MAKE A BEANO
SNOW GLOBE

Show your mates you're a true Beano fan by making this awesome snow globe for your bedroom!

YOU WILL NEED:

- SMALL JAM JAR WITH LID
- GLUE
- SMALL PLASTIC FIGURE OR BOARD GAME PIECE
- WATER
- GLYCERINE
- SPOON
- GLITTER

1 TAKE A SMALL JAR WITH A LID (A JAM JAR IS PERFECT). CLEAN OUT THE INSIDE AND REMOVE ALL LABELS.

2 ON THE INSIDE OF THE LID, GLUE DOWN SMALL OBJECTS LIKE FIGURES OR OLD BOARD GAME PIECES. USE STRONG GLUE SO NOTHING WILL COME LOOSE INSIDE THE JAR!

3 FILL THE JAR ALMOST TO THE TOP WITH WATER AND ADD A DROP OR TWO OF GLYCERINE (ASK AN ADULT TO BUY THIS AT THE SUPERMARKET). NOW, POUR IN A SPOONFUL OF GLITTER.

4 PUT THE LID BACK ON THE FILLED JAR AND SCREW IT SHUT TIGHT. THEN FLIP IT OVER AND GIVE IT A GOOD SHAKE!

IT'S FREEZING IN HERE... AND THAT'S "SNOW" JOKE!

CRAZY PIPE CLEANER
FINGER
PUPPETS

Put on a funny show with these puppets and make your friends laugh their socks off!

YOU WILL NEED:

- PIPE CLEANERS
- MINI POMPOMS OF VARIOUS SIZES
- GLUE
- WHITE CARD
- COLOURING PENS OR PENCILS
- GOOGLY EYES
- SCISSORS
- WIRE CUTTERS (OPTIONAL)
- ADULT HELP

1 WIND A PIPE CLEANER AROUND YOUR FINGER TO MAKE EACH PUPPET'S BODY. LEAVE THE TOP STICKING UP, LIKE A NECK, SO YOU CAN ATTACH THE HEAD.

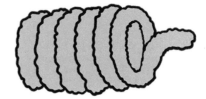

2 TWIST MORE PIPE CLEANERS TO MAKE ARMS, LEGS, HANDS AND FEET (AS SHOWN BELOW), THEN ATTACH THEM TO THE PUPPET'S BODY. DAB SOME GLUE ON THE END OF THE NECK AND PUSH THE POMPOM HEAD DOWN ONTO IT, THEN GLUE ON A TINY POMPOM BUTTON.

3 COMPLETE YOUR PUPPET BY ATTACHING A SMALL POMPOM NOSE AND GOOGLY EYES. ALL DONE!

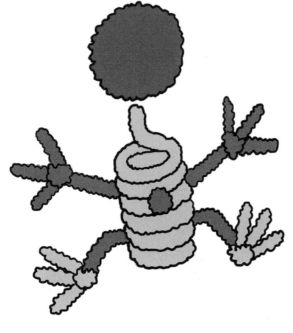

4 HERE ARE SOME OTHER IDEAS FOR YOUR PUPPET SHOW CAST. YOU COULD DRAW FEATURES AND ACCESSORIES ON CARD, THEN COLOUR THEM IN AND ASK AN ADULT TO HELP YOU CUT THEM OUT.

5 NOW TELL JOKES, MAKE FUNNY NOISES AND PUT ON A TOTALLY CRAZY PUPPET SHOW!

SAFETY FIRST!
Pipe cleaners can be tricky to cut, so make sure you always ask an adult to cut them with wire cutters!

MINI BOW AND ARROW

Keep your enemies looking over their shoulders with this sneaky mini bow and arrow!

YOU WILL NEED:

- CRAFT STICKS
- COTTON BUDS
- DENTAL FLOSS
- NAIL SCISSORS
- ADULT HELP

1 ASK AN ADULT TO CARVE NOTCHES INTO THE SIDES OF THE CRAFT STICKS WITH THE SCISSORS. WORKING ABOUT 1 CM FROM THE ENDS. YOU NEED A NOTCH ON EACH SIDE, ON BOTH ENDS. YOU SHOULD END UP WITH FOUR NOTCHES ON EACH STICK.

2 PUT YOUR STICKS INTO A CUP OF WARM WATER. LEAVE FOR AN HOUR. THIS WILL SOFTEN THE WOOD, ALLOWING THEM TO BEND.

3 REMOVE THE STICKS FROM THE WATER AND DRY THEM OFF. WRAP DENTAL FLOSS AROUND ONE END OF EACH STICK ABOUT FOUR TIMES. KNOT IN PLACE, LEAVING THE REST OF THE FLOSS TO WRAP AROUND THE OTHER END OF THE STICK.

4 HOLDING THE STICK IN ONE HAND, STRETCH THE DENTAL FLOSS TO THE NOTCH ON THE OTHER END. MAKE SURE THAT YOU KEEP THE FLOSS ON THE SAME SIDE. CAREFULLY BEND THE STICK AS YOU STRETCH THE FLOSS TIGHTLY ACROSS IT.

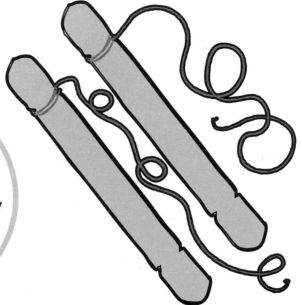

DID YOU KNOW?

An arrow fired from a compound bow can travel up to 200 MPH?

5 WRAP THE FLOSS AROUND THE NOTCH AT THE OTHER END OF THE STICK ABOUT FOUR TIMES AND KNOT IT IN PLACE. YOUR BOW IS READY!

6 TO MAKE THE ARROWS, SIMPLY SNIP ONE END OFF YOUR COTTON BUDS WITH NAIL SCISSORS. ASK AN ADULT TO HELP YOU DO THIS.

7 LINE UP ROWS OF TARGETS TO PRACTISE ON. THEY'LL NEED TO BE SMALL AND LIGHT, SUCH AS TOY FIGURES OR PINE CONES. AS YOU GET BETTER AT HITTING YOUR TARGETS, POSITION THEM FURTHER AND FURTHER AWAY. MAKE SURE YOU NEVER AIM AT A PERSON OR ANIMAL!

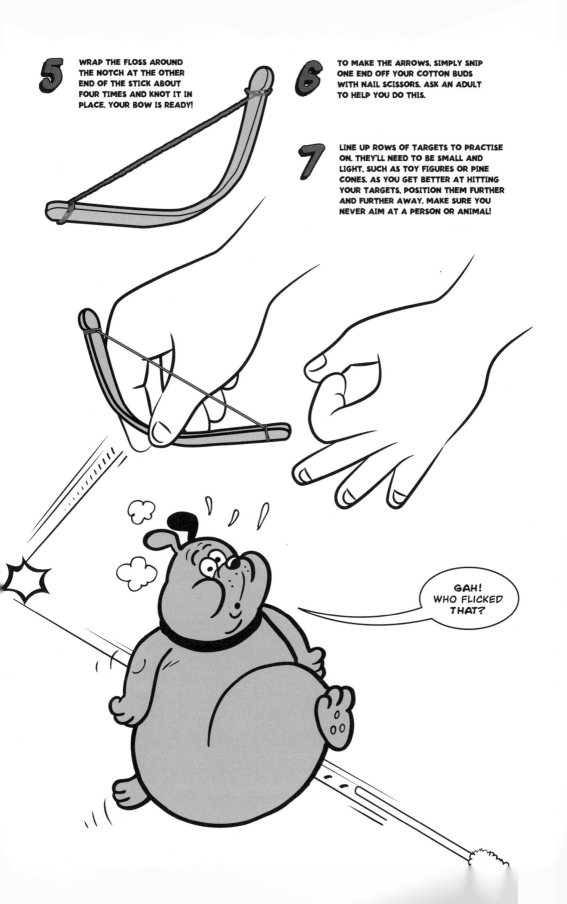

GAH! WHO FLICKED THAT?

BUILD A HANDY
ROBOT STORAGE STACK

This robot might not be able to tidy up your bedroom for you, but it will store all of your craft stuff in one handy place!

YOU WILL NEED:

- 3 SMALL CRISP CARTONS WITH PLASTIC LIDS
- COLOURED OR METALLIC PAPER
- SCISSORS
- STRONG GLUE
- WHITE PAPER
- MARKER PENS
- THIN CARD
- METALLIC STICKERS OR SMALL METAL OBJECTS, SUCH AS BOTTLE TOPS, BUTTONS, BOLTS, WASHERS, NUTS, RING PULLS, PIECES FROM BROKEN TOYS

 1 WIPE OUT THE INSIDES OF THE CRISP CARTONS TO REMOVE ANY GREASE OR SALT. COVER THE OUTSIDE OF THE CARTONS WITH PAPER, THEN STACK THEM ON TOP OF EACH OTHER AND GLUE THEM IN PLACE.

 2 CUT OUT A SQUARE OF WHITE PAPER THAT WILL FIT ON THE CENTRE CARTON AND DRAW A CONTROL PANEL, INCLUDING CIRCUITS, COGS AND DIALS. YOU COULD INCLUDE STICKERS AND PIECES OF RECYCLED METAL GLUE THE PANEL ONTO THE CARTON!

A ROBOT ARMY ON THE LOOSE?!

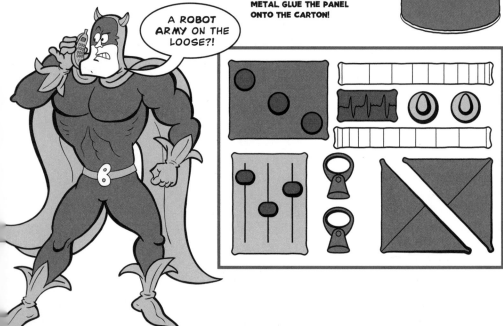

THESE ROBOTS ARE PERFECT FOR MY DIABOLICAL PLANS!

USE RECYCLED MATERIALS TO MAKE A FACE AND ARMS FOR YOUR ROBOT (OR MAKE THEM FROM CARD). IF YOU HAVE SOME WHEELS FROM AN OLD TOY, YOU COULD GLUE THESE TO THE BOTTOM.

TOP TIP: Tall cartons are great for storing your pencils or paintbrushes!

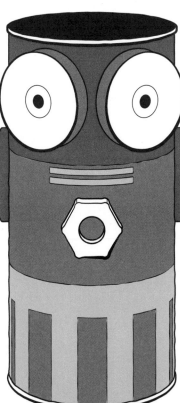

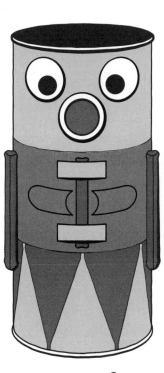

4 HERE ARE SOME MORE GREAT IDEAS FOR DECORATING YOUR ROBOT!

MAKE A FLIPTASTIC
FLIP BOOK

Once you've mastered making a flip book, use it to doodle your sneaky plans in!

YOU WILL NEED:
- A PAD OF STICKY NOTES
- A PENCIL
- AN ERASER
- A MARKER PEN
- A BULLDOG CLIP (OPTIONAL)

1 START WITH A SIMPLE SUBJECT, SUCH AS A BOUNCING BALL. DRAW IT IN PENCIL FIRST AND BEGIN AT THE BACK OF THE BOOK, SO YOU CAN SEE THE PREVIOUS DRAWING THROUGH THE PAPER.

2 DRAW THE OBJECT IN A SLIGHTLY DIFFERENT POSITION ON EACH PAGE. NOW GO OVER YOUR DRAWINGS WITH MARKER PEN WHEN YOU'RE HAPPY WITH HOW THEY LOOK.

3 PUT A BULLDOG CLIP AT THE TOP OF THE PAD TO STOP IT COMING APART, OR HOLD IT TIGHTLY AT THE TOP, AND START FLICKING!

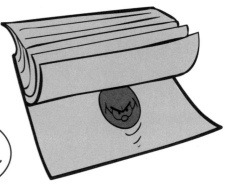

THIS IS A FLIPPING BRILLIANT IDEA, GNASHER!

TOP TIP:
Add moving arms, legs and a head to your bouncing ball to turn it into a jumping man!

SPLAT THE RAT!

Give your mum a fright by leaving loads of these pests around the house – then get SPLATTING!

YOU WILL NEED:

- AN OLD SOCK
- DRIED PEAS, BEANS OR RICE
- STRING
- A LONG CARDBOARD OR PLASTIC TUBE
- A LARGE PIECE OF STRONG CARDBOARD OR WOOD
- TAPE
- A ROLL OF NEWSPAPER

1 FILL THE SOCK WITH DRIED PEAS, BEANS OR RICE. TIE THE OPEN END WITH STRING, LEAVING A PIECE TO MAKE A TAIL. DECORATE THE SOCK TO LOOK LIKE A RAT!

2 TAPE THE TUBE FIRMLY TO THE CARDBOARD OR WOOD, LEAVING ABOUT 75 CM FREE AT THE BOTTOM.

3 MAKE A "SPLATTER" STICK BY ROLLING UP A NEWSPAPER AND FASTENING IT WITH STICKY TAPE. PROP THE CARDBOARD OR WOOD UP AGAINST A WALL AND DROP THE RAT INTO THE TOP OF THE TUBE. THE OTHER PLAYER SHOULD TRY TO SPLAT IT BEFORE IT HITS THE FLOOR!

MARBLED PAPER

Listen up, you lot! Marbled paper is great for wrapping gifts or making greetings cards. Just be sure to ask the owner of the shaving cream before you use it all!

YOU WILL NEED:
- A LARGE TRAY OR ROASTING TIN
- SHAVING FOAM
- A RULER OR SPATULA
- FOOD COLOURING OR PAINT
- A WOODEN STICK (SUCH AS A CHOPSTICK, FOR EXAMPLE)
- HEAVY WHITE PAPER
- KITCHEN TOWEL
- PLENTY OF NEWSPAPER TO KEEP THE TABLE CLEAN

1 SQUIRT A SMALL AMOUNT OF SHAVING FOAM INTO A TRAY OR TIN AND SPREAD IT OUT USING THE RULER OR SPATULA. YOU NEED A THIN LAYER, JUST A BIT BIGGER THAN YOUR SHEET OF PAPER. NOT TOO MUCH, NOW!

2 DRIP EVENLY SPACED DROPS OF FOOD COLOURING OR PAINT ONTO THE SHAVING FOAM. WHAT A MESS!

3 USE THE STICK TO SWIRL THE COLOURS TOGETHER, SO THEY MAKE STREAKS IN THE SHAVING FOAM. DON'T MIX IT UP TOO MUCH – YOU WANT THE COLOURS TO STAY SEPARATE.

4 CAREFULLY LAY THE PAPER ON THE SHAVING FOAM, PRESSING IT DOWN GENTLY AND EVENLY.

 5 LIFT THE PAPER AND LAY IT PAINTED SIDE UP ON SOME KITCHEN TOWEL.

6 USE THE RULER OR SPATULA TO SCRAPE OFF THE SHAVING FOAM, LEAVING THE PAINT BEHIND. NOW LEAVE THE MARBLED PAPER TO DRY.

WHO PINCHED MY SHAVING FOAM?

7 ONCE THE MARBLED PAPER IS DRY, YOU COULD USE IT TO MAKE AN ANCIENT MAP TO FIND BURIED TREASURE OR WRITE A CRAZY LETTER TO A FRIEND!

TOP TIP:
If your paper curls as it dries, try putting a weighted baking tray on top to *flatten it out!*

MARSHMALLOW CATAPULT

You only need five marshmallows to make this totally amazing catapult – which should leave plenty more for scoffing!

YOU WILL NEED:

- PACK OF LARGE MARSHMALLOWS
- 7 WOODEN KEBAB SKEWERS
- A PLASTIC SPOON
- MASKING TAPE
- A THIN RUBBER BAND

1 MAKE A TRIANGLE SHAPE BY STICKING THE ENDS OF THREE SKEWERS INTO THREE MARSHMALLOWS.

2 USE THREE MORE SKEWERS AND ANOTHER MARSHMALLOW TO MAKE A PYRAMID.

3 TAPE THE PLASTIC SPOON FIRMLY ONTO ANOTHER SKEWER.

THAT'S THE COOLEST THING EVER!

YUM! MARSHMALLOWS ARE MY FAVE SWEETS!

4 LOOP THE ELASTIC BAND OVER THE TOP MARSHMALLOW.

5 SLIDE THE SKEWER HOLDING THE SPOON THROUGH THE ELASTIC BAND AND STICK THE END INTO THE MARSHMALLOW OPPOSITE, AT THE BASE.

6 PLACE THE LAST MARSHMALLOW ON THE SPOON AND PULL IT BACK GENTLY, THEN LET GO. YOU MAY NEED TO HOLD ONTO THE BASE AT THE OPPOSITE SIDE UNTIL THE MARSHMALLOWS HAVE HARDENED UP. KA-POW!

TOP TIP: Make a paper target to practise your aiming!

NO WAY! I'M GOING TO EAT THEM FIRST!

SUPER SKETCH

Create your own amazing doodle and show everyone you're the greatest artist in the world!

YOU WILL NEED:
- PENCIL OR PEN
- BLANK SHEET OF PAPER
- COLOURED PENS OR PENCILS

1 START IN ONE CORNER. MOVE YOUR PENCIL AROUND THE PAGE, CREATING BIG LOOPS AND WAVES.

2 DON'T STOP. KEEP THE LINE GOING – ROUND, ALONG, UP, DOWN – UNTIL YOU'VE FILLED THE PAGE WITH A CRAZY PATTERN!

3 GRAB SOME COLOURED PENCILS AND FILL IN THE SHAPES YOU'VE MADE WITH YOUR LINE. GENIUS!

WOW! IT LOOKS JUST LIKE ME...

GLOVE MONSTERS

Use old gloves to make these creepy finger monsters – and scare your mates!

YOU WILL NEED:
- WOOLLEN GLOVES
- POLYESTER OR NEWSPAPER
- FABRIC GLUE OR A NEEDLE AND THREAD
- SCISSORS
- BUTTONS
- SCRAPS OF FELT AND WOOL

1 TO MAKE FOUR-LEGGED MONSTERS, PUSH STUFFING INTO THE FINGERS, THEN PUSH THE THUMB INSIDE THE GLOVE.

2 FILL THE REST OF THE GLOVE WITH STUFFING AND TURN THE CUFF INSIDE. STICK OR SEW IT IN PLACE.

3 DECORATE YOUR MONSTERS WITH BUTTONS, FELT AND PIECES OF WOOL!

WHICH EVIL FIEND STOLE MY SPARE GLOVE?

TOP TIP:
If there are holes in some of the fingers, push them inside and make an **upside-down monster with horns** instead!

DRAW YOUR OWN BEANO
COMIC BOOK

Grab your pencils, pens and paper, then get ready to become an AWESOME Beano comic artist!

YOU WILL NEED:

- A PENCIL OR PENS
- PLAIN PAPER
- AN ERASER

1 COMICS ARE MADE UP OF LOTS OF BOXES CALLED PANELS. THEY'RE READ FROM LEFT TO RIGHT, UNTIL NO PANELS ARE LEFT IN THE ROW, THEN YOU DROP DOWN TO THE NEXT ROW BELOW.

2 SQUARE BOXES (OR INTRO PANELS) AT THE TOP ARE USED TO GUIDE READERS THROUGH THE STORY.

3 THOUGHT BUBBLES SHOW WHAT CHARACTERS ARE THINKING...

4 SPEECH BUBBLES ARE USED TO SHOW WHAT IS ACTUALLY BEING SAID, WITH THE STEM (OR TAIL) POINTING TO WHO'S TALKING.

5 TIME PASSES BETWEEN EACH PANEL. THIS CAN BE SECONDS, DAYS, MONTHS OR EVEN YEARS!

6 USE SOUND EFFECTS AND FLASHES TO ADD EXCITEMENT TO A PANEL!

BOOM!

7 VARY YOUR DRAWINGS WITH CLOSE-UPS AND ZOOMING IN AND OUT OF A SCENE.

8 NOT ALL PANELS HAVE TO BE BOX-SHAPED. THEY COULD BE ROUND, FOR EXAMPLE.

If you aren't that confident at drawing, you could start making comics by painting your finger!

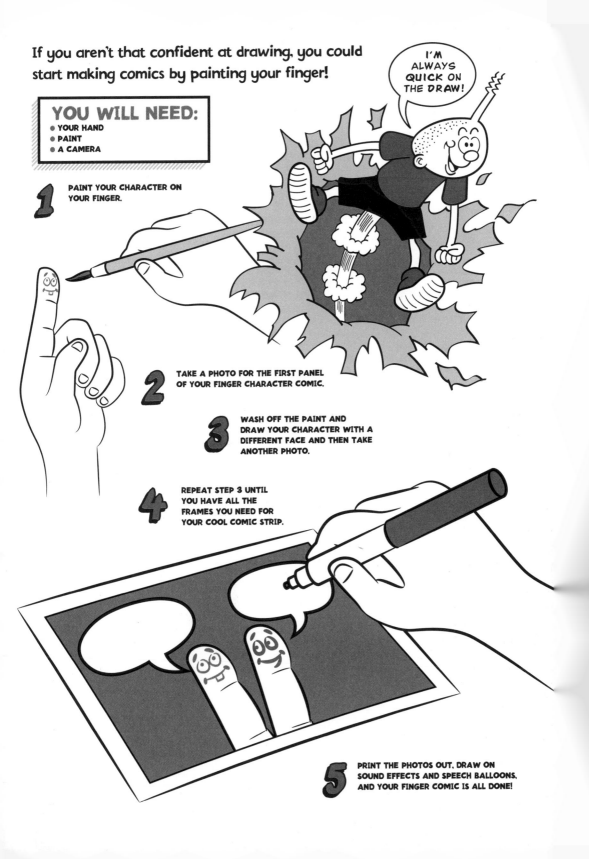

YOU WILL NEED:
● YOUR HAND
● PAINT
● A CAMERA

1 PAINT YOUR CHARACTER ON YOUR FINGER.

I'M ALWAYS QUICK ON THE DRAW!

2 TAKE A PHOTO FOR THE FIRST PANEL OF YOUR FINGER CHARACTER COMIC.

3 WASH OFF THE PAINT AND DRAW YOUR CHARACTER WITH A DIFFERENT FACE AND THEN TAKE ANOTHER PHOTO.

4 REPEAT STEP 3 UNTIL YOU HAVE ALL THE FRAMES YOU NEED FOR YOUR COOL COMIC STRIP.

5 PRINT THE PHOTOS OUT, DRAW ON SOUND EFFECTS AND SPEECH BALLOONS, AND YOUR FINGER COMIC IS ALL DONE!

YUCKY SLIME

Leave this sticky slime in the bath or sink to gross out your parents!

YOU WILL NEED:

- LIQUID LAUNDRY DETERGENT
- LARGE MIXING BOWL AND A SPOON
- 500 ML WHITE OR CLEAR GLUE
- FOOD COLOURING
- RUBBER GLOVES
- A PROTECTIVE COVER FOR THE TABLE
- A HELPFUL ADULT

1 POUR THE GLUE INTO A LARGE MIXING BOWL. ADD SOME DROPS OF FOOD COLOURING AND MIX WELL WITH A SPOON. GIVE IT REALLY FAST STIR!

2 ADD A SMALL DROP OF LAUNDRY DETERGENT AND MIX WELL. CARRY ON MIXING IN SMALL AMOUNTS OF DETERGENT UNTIL THE MIXTURE STARTS TO COME OFF THE SIDES OF THE BOWL.

3 USE YOUR HANDS TO KNEAD THE MIXTURE FOR AT LEAST FIVE MINUTES, UNTIL IT TURNS INTO A SLIME CONSISTENCY (SOLID, STRETCHY AND SO IT DOESN'T STICK TO YOUR FINGERS). YUCK!

SAFETY FIRST!

ASK AN ADULT TO HANDLE THE LAUNDRY DETERGENT, AND WEAR OLD CLOTHES AND GLOVES. USE A PROTECTIVE COVER ON TABLES. DISINFECT AND WASH ALL SURFACES AND MIXING TOOLS WHEN YOU'RE FINISHED. WASH YOUR HANDS AFTER PLAYING WITH SLIME... AND NEVER EAT THE SLIME!

TOP TIP:

Once you've mastered making basic slime, try adding some iron filings to make awesome magnetic slime!

MAKE QUICKSAND

This mushy quicksand mixture works just like the real thing. Be careful you don't make too much – and get sucked into it!

YOU WILL NEED:
- 450 G CORNFLOUR
- 475 ML WATER
- LARGE MIXING BOWL
- SPOON

1 MIX THE CORNFLOUR AND WATER TOGETHER IN THE BOWL. STIR IT SLOWLY AND DRIP IT FROM THE SPOON TO PROVE IT'S A LIQUID.

2 TRY PUNCHING THE MIXTURE, MAKING SURE YOU PULL YOUR FIST BACK QUICKLY! YOU WOULD EXPECT IT TO SPLASH, BUT IT'LL ACTUALLY TURN HARD. YOUR FIST MAKES THE WATER FLOW AWAY, LEAVING A SOLID PATCH OF CORNFLOUR.

3 SCOOP SOME OF THE MIXTURE INTO YOUR HAND AND ROLL IT INTO A BALL. AS LONG AS YOU'RE PRESSING ON IT, THE BALL WILL STAY SOLID, BUT WHEN YOU STOP IT WILL TRICKLE BACK INTO THE BOWL AS A LIQUID. AMAZING!

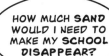

HOW MUCH **SAND** WOULD I NEED TO MAKE MY **SCHOOL** DISAPPEAR?

DRAW A
DINOSAUR

CHECK OUT MY PET DINO-DRAW!

Make a Menace-saur using this Jurassic chart and dice. First, take a blank sheet of paper. Starting with the dinosaur's head, roll the dice to show you which body part to draw next!

	HEADS AND BODIES!	ARMS!	LEGS!	EYES!	MOUTHS!	TAILS!
⚀						
⚁						
⚂						
⚃						
⚄						
⚅						

DRAW A
ZOMBIE

It's time to try your hand at drawing this brain-munching ghoul. Mmm... brains...

'NHHH' LOOKS LIKE IT'S **BRAINS** FOR **TEA** AGAIN, **GNASHER**! 'NHHH'

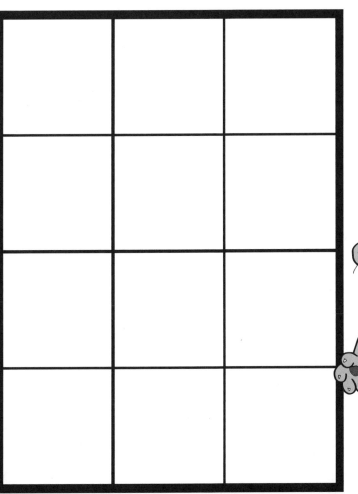

OUT-OF-THIS-WORLD
ASTRO ORBITER

Show your classmates you're a proper brainbox by making this cosmic solar system model!

YOU WILL NEED:

- A ROUND PIECE OF CARDBOARD ABOUT 30 CM IN DIAMETER (E.G. FROM A FROZEN PIZZA BOX)
- A HOLE PUNCH
- A COMPASS
- PENCIL, CRAYONS OR MARKERS
- DIFFERENT-COLOURED CARD
- SCISSORS
- STRING
- A RULER

1 USE THE RULER TO FIND THE CENTRE OF THE CIRCLE OF CARD AND DRAW LINES ACROSS THE MIDDLE, FROM TOP TO BOTTOM AND LEFT TO RIGHT. THEN USE THE HOLE PUNCH TO MAKE FOUR HOLES THROUGH THE LINES, NEAR THE EDGE OF THE CIRCLE. MIND THOSE FINGERS!

2 USING THE COMPASS, DRAW A CIRCLE 4 CM FROM THE CENTRE, THEN DRAW THREE CIRCLES 1 CM APART. THESE FOUR CIRCLES ARE THE ORBITS OF THE ROCKY PLANETS MERCURY, VENUS, EARTH AND MARS.

3 LEAVE A GAP OF 3 CM. THIS IS THE ASTEROID BELT. THEN DRAW FOUR MORE CIRCLES EACH 1 CM APART. THESE FOUR CIRCLES ARE THE ORBITS OF THE GAS GIANTS JUPITER AND SATURN, AND THE ICE GIANTS URANUS AND NEPTUNE.

I'VE GOT A SNEAKY IDEA. I JUST NEED TO PLAN-IT!

4 CUT CIRCLES OF COLOURED CARD FOR THE SUN AND THE PLANETS. THE SUN IS HUGE, SO MAKE IT THE BIGGEST. THE PLANETS IN ORDER OF SIZE FROM THE SMALLEST TO THE LARGEST ARE MERCURY, MARS, VENUS, EARTH, NEPTUNE, URANUS, SATURN AND JUPITER. MAKE A HOLE IN THE TOP OF EACH CIRCLE WITH THE HOLE PUNCH.

 5 MAKE A HOLE WITH THE COMPASS POINT IN THE CENTRE OF THE CIRCLE AND SOMEWHERE IN EACH OF THE ORBITS, SO THE PLANETS WILL BE WELL-SPACED.

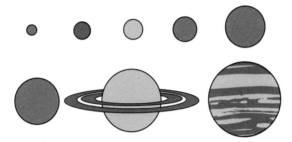

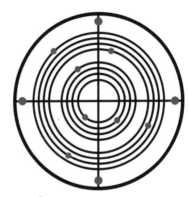

6 TIE STRING THROUGH THE HOLE IN THE SUN AND THREAD THE OTHER END THROUGH THE HOLE IN THE CENTRE OF THE CIRCLE, THEN TIE A KNOT. DO THE SAME WITH THE PLANETS, ATTACHING THEM TO THEIR MATCHING ORBITS.

7 CUT FOUR PIECES OF STRING ABOUT 20 CM IN LENGTH AND TIE A PIECE THROUGH EACH OF THE FOUR HOLES AT THE EDGE OF THE CARDBOARD CIRCLE. TIE THE ENDS TOGETHER AT THE TOP OF THE CIRCLE, SO IT IS EVENLY BALANCED AND THEN HANG UP YOUR MOBILE. FINISHED!

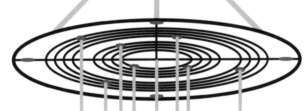

DID YOU KNOW?

Our solar system was formed around 4.6 billion years ago. That's older than your teacher!

EGGS-TREME EGGS

You can use a clean shell for these Beano heads. Remember to scoop their eggy brains out first!

YOU WILL NEED:
- EGGS AT ROOM TEMPERATURE
- A SHARP OBJECT, SUCH AS A NEEDLE OR THE POINT OF A COMPASS
- A DRINKING STRAW
- A BOWL
- FOOD COLOURING
- VINEGAR
- OPTIONAL: ELASTIC BANDS, FELT PENS, STICKERS, GOOGLY EYES, STICK-ON JEWELS, RIBBON, TAPE, ETC.

1 CLEAN THE OUTSIDE OF THE EGGSHELL BY HOLDING IT UNDER THE TAP, THEN LEAVE IT TO DRY.

2 ASK AN ADULT TO MAKE A HOLE IN THE LARGER, END OF THE EGG WITH A SHARP OBJECT. SLOWLY MAKE THE HOLE BIGGER, SO THE YUMMY YOLK CAN PASS THROUGH. POKE AROUND IN THE HOLE TO MIX THE EGG UP, THEN MAKE A SMALLER HOLE IN THE OTHER END OF THE EGG.

TOP TIP:
Don't waste the eggs! Use them to make omelettes, scrambled eggs or cakes. **SLURP!**

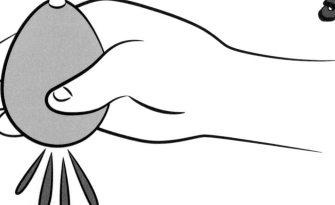

3 HOLD THE LARGER HOLE OVER A BOWL AND PLACE A DRINKING STRAW ON TOP OF THE SMALLER HOLE. BLOW THROUGH THE SMALLER HOLE UNTIL THE EGG IS EMPTY.

4 COLOUR THE EGGS BY DIPPING THEM IN A GLASS HALF FILLED WITH HOT WATER, A TEASPOON OF FOOD COLOURING AND A TEASPOON OF VINEGAR. YOU CAN CREATE STRIPES, SPOTS OR OTHER PATTERNS ON YOUR EGGS BY PLACING ELASTIC BANDS OR STICKERS ON THE EGGS BEFORE YOU DIP THEM.

5 NOW IT'S TIME TO GET CREATIVE! TRY DECORATING YOUR EGGS AS YOUR FAVE BEANO CHARACTERS. GET CRACKING!!

MAKE YOUR OWN
PAPER SAMURAI WARRIOR'S HAT

Make some of these helmets for your mates and start your own samurai warrior clan!

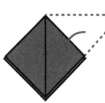

YOU WILL NEED:
- A PIECE OF PAPER ABOUT 50 CM SQUARE
- SCISSORS
- PAINTS, MARKERS OR CRAYONS

1 FOLD THE PAPER IN HALF DIAGONALLY TO MAKE A TRIANGLE WITH THE FOLD AT THE TOP, THEN FOLD BOTH THE TOP CORNERS OF THE TRIANGLE OVER SO THEY TOUCH THE BOTTOM CORNER.

2 FOLD BOTH THE TOP AND BOTTOM TIPS UP SO THEY TOUCH THE TOP CORNER.

3 NOW FOLD THE TIPS OUTWARDS AS SHOWN.

DID YOU KNOW?

The word "samurai" means "one who serves". Children trained to be samurais from the age of five!

I'M OFF FOR A SAMU-RIDE!

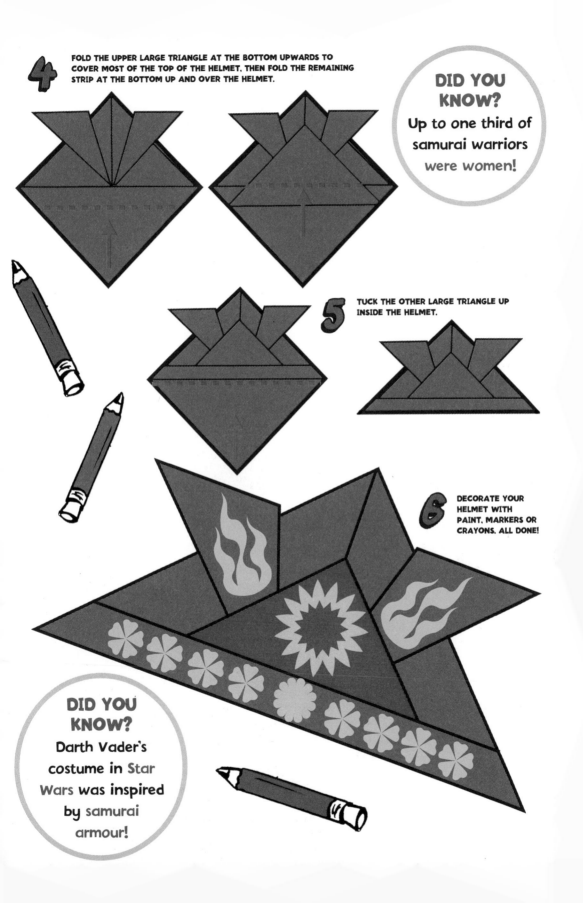

4 FOLD THE UPPER LARGE TRIANGLE AT THE BOTTOM UPWARDS TO COVER MOST OF THE TOP OF THE HELMET, THEN FOLD THE REMAINING STRIP AT THE BOTTOM UP AND OVER THE HELMET.

DID YOU KNOW?
Up to one third of samurai warriors were women!

5 TUCK THE OTHER LARGE TRIANGLE UP INSIDE THE HELMET.

6 DECORATE YOUR HELMET WITH PAINT, MARKERS OR CRAYONS. ALL DONE!

DID YOU KNOW?
Darth Vader's costume in Star Wars was inspired by samurai armour!

MAKE A MACARONI
MONSTER

Pasta's not just for scoffing, y'know! Try gluing pasta shapes to make a super scary monster fridge magnet or creepy-creature badge!

YOU WILL NEED:

- PLASTIC ZIPLOCK SANDWICH BAGS
- VINEGAR
- FOOD COLOURING
- DRIED PASTA SHAPES, E.G. MACARONI, PENNE, FUSILLI
- PAPER TOWELS OR NEWSPAPER
- STRONG GLUE
- GOOGLY EYES
- NAME BADGES OR FRIDGE MAGNETS

1 PUT THE PASTA INTO PLASTIC SANDWICH BAGS, USING A DIFFERENT BAG FOR EACH COLOUR. ADD THREE OR FOUR TABLESPOONS OF VINEGAR AND SEVERAL DROPS OF FOOD COLOURING. NOW SEAL THE BAG TIGHTLY AND SHAKE IT WELL UNTIL THE PASTA IS ALL COLOURED.

2 OPEN THE BAG A LITTLE AND POUR THE LIQUID AWAY. LAY THE PASTA ON LAYERS OF PAPER TOWELS OR NEWSPAPER TO DRY.

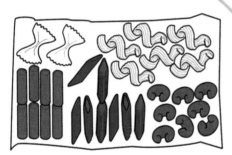

3 ONCE DRY, GLUE THE PASTA TOGETHER TO MAKE MONSTER SHAPES AND THEN ATTACH THE EYES.

4 TRY MAKING ALL SORTS OF CRAZY CREATURES USING THE DIFFERENT PASTA SHAPES!

MAKE A PAPER
HELICOPTER

You can have awesome paper helicopter races with your mates! How far can you make yours spin?

YOU WILL NEED:
- A STRIP OF PAPER ABOUT 4 CM WIDE AND 11 CM LONG
- RULER
- PENCIL
- SCISSORS
- PAPER CLIP

1 DRAW TWO VERTICAL LINES 5 CM FROM EACH END OF THE PAPER.

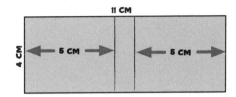

2 DRAW A LINE ACROSS THE CENTRE OF THE RIGHT-HAND SIDE AND CUT ALONG IT. DRAW TWO LINES TO DIVIDE THE LEFT-HAND SIDE INTO THREE.

3 FOLLOWING THE RED ARROWS, CUT ONE THIRD IN FROM THE EDGES OF THE PAPER ON EACH SIDE. FOLD THE SIDES OVER INTO THE MIDDLE TO MAKE ONE CENTRAL STRIP.

4 FOLD UP THE BOTTOM QUARTER OF THE CENTRAL STRIP AND HOLD IT IN PLACE WITH THE PAPER CLIP. FOLD ONE OF THE TOP FLAPS FORWARDS AND THE OTHER BACKWARDS. NOW RELEASE YOUR HELICOPTER AND THEN WATCH IT SPIN!

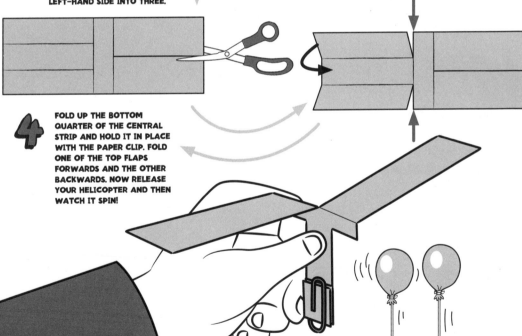

HA! NO ONE WILL CATCH ME PRANKING FROM UP HERE!

BOOKS EVERY KID SHOULD READ!

Who says reading is boring? Here's our top picks for books that every Menace should definitely check out!

CHARLIE AND THE CHOCOLATE FACTORY
Roald Dahl

THIS IS MY FAVE BOOK! WHO WOULDN'T WANT TO SCOFF ALL OF THOSE YUMMY SWEETS?!

HARRY POTTER SERIES
J.K. Rowling

YOU SHOULD READ ALL OF THESE MAGICAL BOOKS, AS THEY STAR A HERO AS HANDSOME AS ME!

THE LORD OF THE RINGS
J.R.R. Tolkien

I'M GOING FOR THE LORD OF THE RINGS, AS THERE ARE BIG, SCARY, HAIRY SPIDERS IN IT!

WHERE THE WILD THINGS ARE
Maurice Sendak

I'M ALWAYS GOING CRAZY, STOMPING AROUND AND BEING A MONSTER, JUST LIKE THIS FURRY BUNCH!

THE WIND IN THE WILLOWS
Kenneth Grahame

I LIKE THE CHARACTER OF TOAD IN THIS BOOK - BECAUSE HE'S ALWAYS HAVING ACCIDENTS!

THE NEVERENDING STORY
Michael Ende

THIS BOOK IS GREAT, BUT THERE'S ACTUALLY A LAST PAGE - I THOUGHT IT WAS NEVERENDING?!

JAMES AND THE GIANT PEACH
Roald Dahl

THIS BOOK IS SUPER FUN. THERE'S A GIANT FRUIT IN IT, MAKING IT AN EVEN TASTIER READ!

A SERIES OF UNFORTUNATE EVENTS
Lemony Snicket

HEH, HEH! MAYBE SNEAKY COUNT OLAF COULD HELP ME DEFEAT BANANAMAN ONCE AND FOR ALL...

THE BFG
Roald Dahl

I THINK MY LONG, STRIPY TIE MIGHT ACTUALLY BE A LITTLE TOO SHORT FOR THE BFG TO WEAR!

LITTLE WOMEN
Louisa May Alcott

THERE'S SOMETHING ABOUT THE TITLE OF THIS BOOK I REALLY LIKE, BUT I'M NOT SURE WHAT IT IS?

THIS IS MY FAVOURITE BOOK OF ALL TIME!

TREASURE ISLAND
Robert Louis Stevenson

I BET I COULD FIND ALL OF THE BURIED PIRATE TREASURE IN THIS BOOK SUPERFAST!

THE CAT IN THE HAT
Dr Seuss

THIS BOOK ALWAYS REMINDS ME OF A NAUGHTY PRANK I ONCE PLAYED ON MY MUM!

A LITTLE PRINCESS
Frances Hodgson Burnett

THIS IS MY FAVE BOOK – BECAUSE I'M A LITTLE PRINCESS, TOO. THHRRRP!

THE BORROWERS
Mary Norton

I BORROW ALL SORTS OF STUFF FROM MY DAD – I JUST ALWAYS FORGET TO GIVE IT BACK!

DENNIS AND THE CHAMBER OF MISCHIEF
Nigel Auchterlounie

GNEE-HEE! CHECK OUT WHAT HAPPENS WHEN I MEET A GIANT GNASHERSAURUS-REX!

OUTDOOR FUN!

If you want to be a real Minx or Menace, it's time to get outside and try out these awesome activities! It doesn't matter if it's rain or shine – grab some mates and get ready to get mucky...

WATER CUP RACE

Grab your water pistols and battle it out to see who'll be the water cup-race champion. Ready, steady... GET BLASTING!

YOU WILL NEED:

- PLASTIC CUPS
- STRING
- BUCKET
- WATER PISTOLS

1 ASK AN ADULT TO HELP YOU MAKE HOLES IN THE BOTTOM OF SOME PLASTIC CUPS.

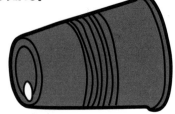

2 TIE ONE END OF A PIECE OF STRING TO A POST OR A TREE – ONE FOR EACH PLAYER. THREAD A CUP ONTO THE STRING, BEFORE TYING THE OTHER END. MAKE SURE THAT EACH PLAYER'S STRING IS THE SAME LENGTH – NO CHEATING!

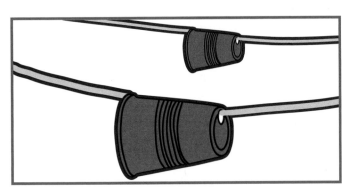

3 PULL THE CUPS TO EQUAL STARTING POSITIONS. PLACE THE BUCKET OF WATER BETWEEN EACH STRING LINE AT THE START. LOAD YOUR WATER PISTOLS, AND RACE YOUR WAY TO THE FINISHING LINE!

TOP TIP:
Try practising on your own using a stopwatch. What's your best race time?

PAPER PLATE
FLYING SAUCERS

Everyone knows I'm the king of frisbee chucking! How far can you throw yours?

YOU WILL NEED:
- 2 PAPER PLATES
- STICKY TAPE
- SCISSORS
- MARKER PENS

1 PLACE THE PLATES RIGHT SIDE UP. COVER THEM WITH STRIPS OF TAPE, LETTING THEM OVERLAP THE EDGES.

2 TRIM AROUND THE EDGE OF EACH PLATE TO REMOVE THE EXTRA TAPE. MAKE A HOLE IN THE CENTRE OF ONE OF THE PLATES. DRAW AROUND A LID OR A SAUCER TO GET A PERFECT CIRCLE. GET AN ADULT TO PIERCE THE CENTRE OF THE CIRCLE WITH SCISSORS AND CUT IT OUT. NOW CUT A HOLE IN THE OTHER PLATE IN THE SAME WAY.

3 TURN THE PLATES OVER AND DECORATE WITH MARKER PENS. COVER THE DECORATED SIDES OF YOUR PLATES WITH TAPE. LET THE TAPE HANG OVER THE SIDES, AND TRIM IT ON ONE PLATE AS BEFORE. LEAVE THE OVERHANGING TAPE ON THE OTHER PLATE AND USE IT TO JOIN THE TWO PLATES TOGETHER. NOW YOU'RE READY FOR LAUNCH!

OVER HERE!

MINI PARACHUTE

How much mischief could you cause if you were able to parachute in anywhere you like? Er... maybe you should practice with an action figure first...

YOU WILL NEED:

- 25 CM SQUARE PIECE OF LIGHTWEIGHT FABRIC
- SCISSORS
- A BUTTON WITH FOUR HOLES
- 2 LENGTHS OF 90 CM THREAD
- SMALL PLASTIC ACTION FIGURES

1 FOLD OVER ONE CORNER OF THE FABRIC AND CAREFULLY SNIP A SMALL HOLE NEAR THE EDGE OF THAT CORNER WITH THE SCISSORS. REPEAT ON THE OTHER THREE SIDES.

2 NOW TAKE ONE OF THE THREADS AND TIE ONE END TO THE CORNER OF THE FABRIC. SIMPLE!

3 TAKE THE OTHER END OF THE THREAD THROUGH ONE BUTTONHOLE, THEN THROUGH THE DIAGONALLY OPPOSITE BUTTONHOLE.

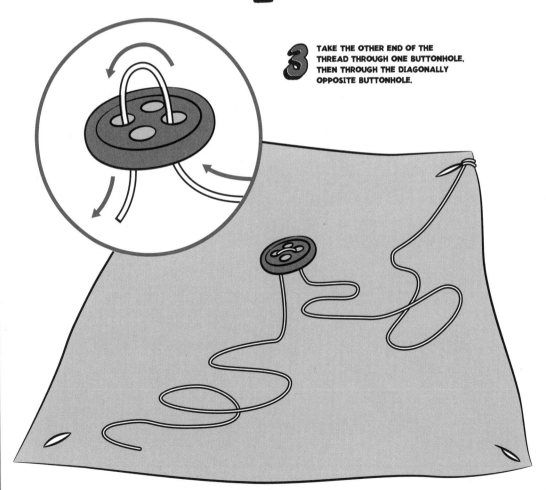

4 PULL THE THREAD UNTIL THE BUTTON IS IN THE MIDDLE AND TIE THE LOOSE END TO THE OPPOSITE CORNER OF THE FABRIC. REPEAT WITH THE OTHER THREAD AND CORNERS.

5 HOLD THE THREADS FROM THE TOP OF THE BUTTON. SLIDE THE BUTTON DOWN ABOUT TWO-THIRDS OF THE THREAD AND THEN TIE A KNOT.

6 TIE AN ACTION FIGURE TO THE END OF THE STRINGS. YOU'RE NOW READY FOR A TEST FLIGHT! LAUNCH THE PARACHUTE BY THROWING IT IN THE AIR OR DROP IT FROM A HEIGHT (SUCH AS A WALL, TREE OR CHAIR) WITH THE HELP OF AN ADULT. WATCH IT GO!

GAH! THIS ISN'T A GOOD TIME TO FIND OUT I'M AFRAID OF HEIGHTS!

ULTIMATE
SAND PALACE

Build a totally awesome sandcastle fit for a real Menace. You'll need loads of wet sand and a bucketful of imagination!

YOU WILL NEED:

- SANDY BEACH OR SANDPIT
- LONG SHOVEL
- RUBBISH BIN WITH NO BOTTOM (GET AN ADULT TO CUT OFF THE BOTTOM)
- A BUCKET WITH NO BOTTOM (AN ADULT WILL NEED TO CUT OFF THE BOTTOM)
- SMALL CONTAINERS
- FUNNEL
- SPRAY BOTTLE
- SCULPTING TOOLS: WHATEVER YOU CAN FIND AT HOME – CAKE DECORATING TOOLS, SPATULAS, MAKE-UP BRUSHES, CRAFT STICKS, PASTRY CUTTERS ARE ALL GREAT
- FLAGS

 1 FIND A GOOD SPOT ON THE BEACH JUST ABOVE THE TIDELINE (WHERE THE DARK SAND BECOMES LIGHTER). USE A SHOVEL TO DIG A CIRCLE IN THE SAND, PILING IT UP INTO THE MIDDLE TO MAKE A HILL. DON'T FORGET TO BEND YOUR KNEES!

 2 STAMP THE TOP OF YOUR HILL INTO A VOLCANO CRATER SHAPE. NOW POUR WATER INTO THE CRATER. USE YOUR FEET TO PUSH THE SAND DOWN. THIS WILL BE THE FOUNDATION FOR YOUR ULTIMATE CREATION!

 3 NEXT, PUT YOUR RUBBISH BIN ON TOP. FILL IT THREE QUARTERS FULL WITH SAND. POUR IN A FEW BUCKETS OF WATER AND PRESS THE SAND DOWN WITH YOUR HANDS OR A BUCKET. ADD MORE SAND AND WATER. KEEP GOING UNTIL THE RUBBISH BIN IS FULL.

I CAN BUILD SANDCASTLES FASTER THAN ANYONE!

PLACE A SMALLER BOTTOMLESS CONTAINER ON TOP. ADD SAND UNTIL IT'S THREE QUARTERS FULL. ADD SOME WATER AND PUSH DOWN, AS IN STEP 3. CONTINUE TO ADD SAND AND FILL THE SMALLER CONTAINERS ON TOP OF ONE ANOTHER.

 CAREFULLY PAT THE SIDES OF THE TOP CONTAINER, THEN VERY SLOWLY PULL IT OFF THE TOP TOWER. RELEASE ALL OF YOUR CONTAINERS IN TURN, FROM THE TOP DOWN.

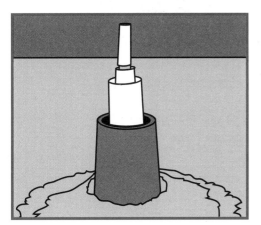

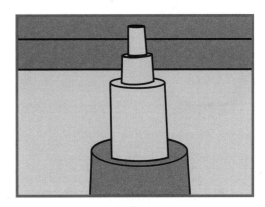

 ADD A TURRET. FILL THE FUNNEL WITH VERY WET SAND AND PUT IT ON YOUR TOP TOWER. SMOOTH THE SAND DOWN. A MAKE-UP BRUSH OR SPATULA IS GOOD FOR THIS. YOU CAN ALSO ADD WET SAND TO FINISH OFF ANY EDGES.

 ALWAYS START CARVING FROM THE TOP DOWN, SO THAT THE SAND FALLS AWAY FROM YOUR FINISHED AREAS. KEEP THE SAND WET WITH YOUR SPRAY BOTTLE. JOIN TOWERS WITH SPIRALLING RAMPS, USING CRAFT STICKS TO MAKE STEPS. CUT ARCHWAYS, DOORWAYS, AND WINDOWS... AND DON'T FORGET TO PUT FLAGS ON THE TOP, TOO!

WOODLAND BASE

Head to the woods with your mates and build this awesome secret den. Remember – no parents allowed inside!

1 FIND SOME OPEN WOODLAND TO BUILD YOUR BASE. LOOK FOR A PLACE WITH FLAT GROUND. FIND TWO STRONG BRANCHES WITH FORKED ENDS FOR UPRIGHTS. THEN PUSH THEM INTO THE GROUND, A COUPLE OF METRES APART, MAKING SURE THEY'RE AT THE SAME HEIGHT.

2 NOW YOU NEED TO FIND A STRONG BRANCH TO SIT ACROSS THE FORKED UPRIGHTS. THIS WILL BE YOUR RIDGE POLE. MAKE SURE THAT YOUR STRUCTURE IS STURDY. IF NOT, DRIVE YOUR UPRIGHTS INTO THE GROUND A LITTLE MORE.

OI! GO GET MORE STICKS!

3 GATHER UP LOTS OF STRONG, LONG STICKS FROM THE WOODLAND FLOOR. ONLY USE DEAD WOOD – DON'T BREAK ANY BRANCHES FROM THE TREES. LEAN THE STICKS UP AGAINST YOUR RIDGE POLE. PLACE THEM EVENLY AGAINST BOTH SIDES. IT'S BEST TO PUT A FEW ON ONE SIDE, THEN A FEW ON THE OTHER, AND SO ON, SO THAT ONE SIDE DOESN'T GET TOO HEAVY AND FALL DOWN!

ALRIGHT DEN!

4 CONTINUE TO ADD STICKS AND BRANCHES UNTIL YOU'VE MADE A TENT-SHAPED STRUCTURE. USE AS MANY STICKS AS POSSIBLE TO FILL IN THE GAPS. YOU CAN EITHER CLOSE OFF ONE END IN THE SAME WAY OR LEAVE BOTH ENDS OPEN.

5 COLLECT LEAVES FROM THE FOREST FLOOR AND PILE THEM UP AGAINST YOUR STRUCTURE. START FROM THE BOTTOM AND WORK YOUR WAY UP. YOU CAN ALSO USE MOSS, PINE NEEDLES OR BRACKEN IF YOU FIND ANY LYING AROUND.

6 WHEN YOU'VE FINISHED, IT'S TIME TO GO INSIDE! IT SHOULD BE SNUG AND WARM IN YOUR WOODLAND BASE – THE PERFECT PLACE TO HIDE FROM YOUR ENEMIES!

MAKE YOUR OWN
LAZY HAMMOCK

Trying to dodge homework or boring chores? Just have a lazy afternoon in the garden with your own hammock!

YOU WILL NEED:

- 1 LARGE BED SHEET (NOT TOO OLD AND WORN. ASK AN ADULT FIRST)
- 2 PIECES OF 60 CM UTILITY CORD (AVAILABLE FROM CLIMBING SHOPS AND HARDWARE STORES)
- 2 PIECES OF 1 METRE WEBBING (AVAILABLE FROM CLIMBING SHOPS AND HARDWARE STORES)
- ADULT HELP

1 TAKE ONE PIECE OF CORD AND MAKE A LOOP AT THE END. SECURE WITH A DOUBLE KNOT. LEAVING A 10 CM "TAIL".

2 LOOSELY ZIGZAG, FOLD OR GATHER YOUR SHEET LENGTHWAYS. THEN FOLD OVER ONE OF THE WIDTH ENDS AT ABOUT 20 CM.

3 GATHER THE FABRIC FROM BOTH SIDES ABOUT 10 CM IN FROM THE EDGE. HOLD WITH YOUR FIST.

I'M STANDING UP!

SAFETY FIRST!

An adult needs to check that your knots are tight enough and hang your hammock up for you. Strong trees, beams and branches are all great places to hang your hammock. Be sure not to hang it too high up!

I RECKON YOU'RE LYING!

4 WRAP THE CORD FROM STEP 1 AROUND THE SHEET WHERE YOUR FIST IS AND THEN THREAD THE LOOSE END THROUGH THE LOOP.

5 PULL THE CORD UNTIL THE LOOP IS TIGHT TO THE SHEET. WRAP THE CORD TIGHTLY AROUND THE SHEET FIVE OR SIX TIMES AND TIE THE ENDS TOGETHER WITH A SECURE DOUBLE KNOT!

6 THREAD ONE PIECE OF WEBBING THROUGH THE END OF YOUR SHEET. TIE A SECURE KNOT IN YOUR WEBBING. REPEAT THESE STEPS ON THE OTHER SIDE.

7 YOUR HAMMOCK IS NOW READY FOR AN ADULT TO HANG UP FOR YOU. ASK THEM TO CHECK THAT YOUR KNOTS ARE SECURE FIRST AND TO TIGHTEN THEM IF NECESSARY. NOW IT'S TIME FOR A LAZY REST. ZZZ...

TOP TIP: While you're snoozing outside, you can be planning your next batch of tricks!

WATER BALLOON BATTLE

Cool off on a scorching hot day and invite your mates to an all-out water balloon fight. Get ready to get wet – VERY wet!

1 BLOW UP EACH BALLOON FIRST AND STRETCH IT A BIT. THIS SHOULD STOP IT FROM POPPING. STRETCH THE NECK OF THE BALLOON OVER THE END OF A TAP OR HOSE. TURN ON A MEDIUM STREAM OF WATER SO IT DOESN'T SHOOT OFF! TURN THE WATER OFF BEFORE THE BALLOON FILLS TO THE TOP.

2 TIE THE BALLOONS TIGHTLY, A FEW CENTIMETRES FROM THE TOP. PUT THEM IN BUCKETS. THIS CAN TAKE A WHILE, SO ASK YOUR FRIENDS TO HELP!

3 DIVIDE YOUR FRIENDS INTO TWO TEAMS. WHEN SOMEONE IS HIT, THE OTHER TEAM SCORES A POINT. TAKE TURNS OR JUST HAVE A CRAZY FREE-FOR-ALL!

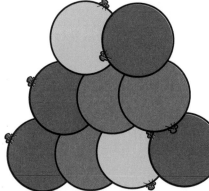

TIME TO MAKE A BIG SPLASH!

STONE SKIMMING

Really impress your mates this summer when you pull off the most epic of stone skims in the history of ever!

1 MAKE SURE YOU CHOOSE AN EPIC-SIZED STONE TO PERFORM AN EPIC SKIM - SKINNY, FLAT, ROUND AND ABOUT THE SIZE OF YOUR PALM.

2 HOLD IT IN YOUR HAND WITH YOUR THUMB ON ONE SIDE AND THE REST OF YOUR FINGERS ON THE OTHER. MAKE SURE THE STONE SITS IN THE CROOK OF YOUR INDEX FINGER.

3 FACE A LAKE OR LARGE POND SIDEWAYS, WITH YOUR FEET SHOULDER-WIDTH APART. MAKE SURE AN ADULT IS WITH YOU AT ALL TIMES.

4 IF YOU'RE RIGHT-HANDED, STAND WITH YOUR LEFT FOOT FACING FORWARDS. IF YOU'RE LEFT-HANDED, STAND WITH YOUR RIGHT FOOT FORWARDS.

5 BEND YOUR WRIST ALL THE WAY BACK AND FLICK IT FORWARDS, RELEASING THE STONE AS YOU DO SO. TRY TO GET THE STONE TO HIT THE WATER AT AN ANGLE OF ABOUT 20 DEGREES FROM THE WATER'S SURFACE.

6 ONCE YOU'VE RELEASED THE STONE FROM YOUR HAND, KEEP MOVING YOUR ARM ACROSS YOUR CHEST TO KEEP THE MOMENTUM GOING. HOW FAR CAN YOU THROW YOURS?

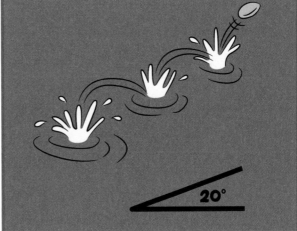

20°

SPOOKY SHADOW-MONSTER SHOW

Put on a spooky shadow show for your mates one evening – it'll be EPIC!

YOU WILL NEED:
- AN OLD SHEET
- A BIG TORCH OR OUTDOOR LAMP
- SKETCHBOOK AND PENCIL
- BLACK CARD
- SCISSORS
- BRASS FASTENERS (SPLIT PINS)
- WOODEN SKEWERS OR A THIN GARDEN CANE
- MASKING TAPE
- WHITE COLOURED PENCIL OR CRAYON
- YOUR IMAGINATION!

1 FIRST, DECIDE ON THE STORY THAT YOU'RE GOING TO PERFORM. IS IT A WELL-KNOWN STORY OR SOMETHING SCARY YOU'VE MADE UP YOURSELF? SKETCH ANY CHARACTERS AND PROPS THAT YOU MIGHT NEED FOR THE SHOW.

2 FOR EACH SHADOW PUPPET CHARACTER, DRAW A HEAD AND BODY ONTO BLACK CARD WITH A PENCIL OR CRAYON. INCLUDE DETAILS SUCH AS EYES, HAIR AND MOUTH.

3 ADD LIMBS. CUT OUT ARMS AND LEGS, AND JOIN THEM TO YOUR CHARACTER'S BODY WITH BRASS FASTENERS (SPLIT PINS). THIS MEANS YOU CAN MAKE THEM MOVE AROUND IN THE SHOW!

DID YOU KNOW?
This type of puppetry is called shadow play and is thought to have started in China thousands of years ago!

4 ATTACH THE SKEWERS TO THE MAIN BODY AND EACH OF THE LIMBS. FIX IN PLACE WITH MASKING TAPE. HOLD THE SKEWERS TO MOVE THE CHARACTERS.

5 HANG THE SHEET UP OUTSIDE — YOU COULD TIE IT TO THE BRANCHES OF A TREE OR BETWEEN TWO POSTS. YOU WILL NEED SPACE IN FRONT FOR THE AUDIENCE AND BEHIND FOR YOU TO SIT WITH THE PUPPETS.

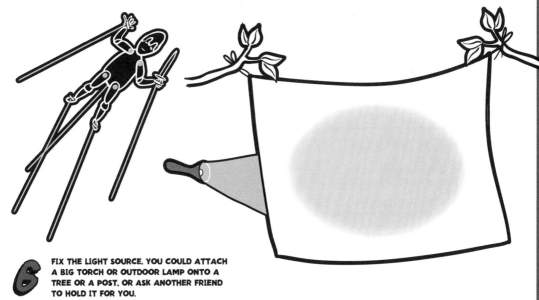

6 FIX THE LIGHT SOURCE. YOU COULD ATTACH A BIG TORCH OR OUTDOOR LAMP ONTO A TREE OR A POST, OR ASK ANOTHER FRIEND TO HOLD IT FOR YOU.

7 NOW INVITE YOUR FRIENDS ROUND, WAIT UNTIL DARK AND PUT ON YOUR SPOOKY SHOW!

MAKE AND FLY A
QUICK KITE

You might not have superpowers like Bananaman, but you can still take to the skies with this awesome flying kite!

YOU WILL NEED:

- BROWN PAPER BAG
- MARKERS, CRAYONS OR PAINTS TO DESIGN AND DECORATE YOUR KITE
- HOLE PUNCH
- 4 PIECES OF STRING 50 CM LONG
- PIECE OF STRING AT LEAST 2.5 M LONG
- STICKY TAPE
- SEVERAL TORN PIECES OF CREPE PAPER 20 CM LONG
- CRAFT STICK OR LOLLYPOP STICK

1 FIRST, GET THE PAPER BAG. DECORATE IT WITH MARKERS AND DOODLE WHATEVER YOU WANT ON IT – EVEN A PIC OF BANANAMAN!

2 OPEN THE PAPER BAG AND PUNCH ONE HOLE AT EACH OF THE FOUR CORNERS AT THE TOP OF THE BAG. THE HOLES SHOULD BE ABOUT 2 CM AWAY FROM THE RIM.

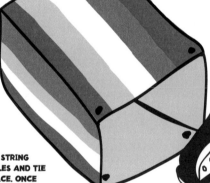

3 PUSH ONE 50 CM PIECE OF STRING THROUGH EACH OF THE HOLES AND TIE A KNOT SO IT STAYS IN PLACE. ONCE YOU'VE ATTACHED ALL FOUR STRINGS, TIE THEIR ENDS TOGETHER AND CONNECT THEM TO YOUR 2.5 M-LONG PIECE OF STRING.

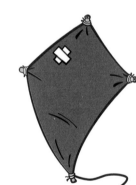

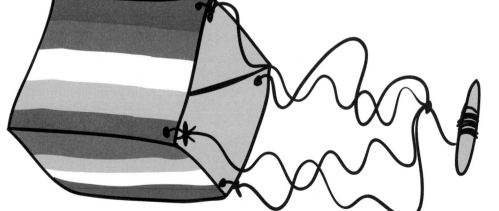

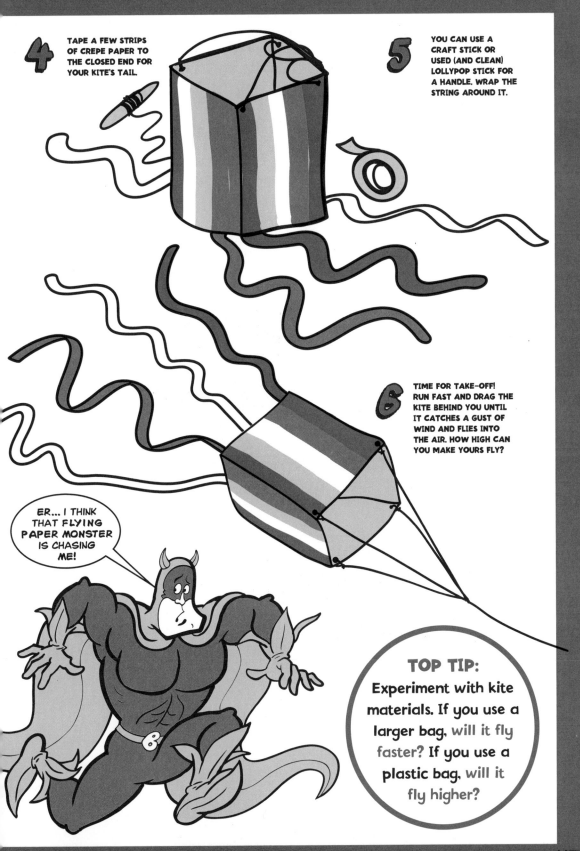

4 TAPE A FEW STRIPS OF CREPE PAPER TO THE CLOSED END FOR YOUR KITE'S TAIL.

5 YOU CAN USE A CRAFT STICK OR USED (AND CLEAN) LOLLYPOP STICK FOR A HANDLE. WRAP THE STRING AROUND IT.

6 TIME FOR TAKE-OFF! RUN FAST AND DRAG THE KITE BEHIND YOU UNTIL IT CATCHES A GUST OF WIND AND FLIES INTO THE AIR. HOW HIGH CAN YOU MAKE YOURS FLY?

ER... I THINK THAT FLYING PAPER MONSTER IS CHASING ME!

TOP TIP: Experiment with kite materials. If you use a larger bag, will it fly faster? If you use a plastic bag, will it fly higher?

SECRET SIGNALS

Use these cool flags to send secret messages to your friends from the other side of a football field (or from the bottom of your garden)!

YOU WILL NEED:

- 2 SHEETS OF THICK YELLOW PAPER
- 2 SHEETS OF THICK RED PAPER
- PAPER GLUE
- RULER
- PENCIL
- SCISSORS
- 2 DOWELS OR FLOWER STICKS
- ADHESIVE TAPE
- NOTEBOOK AND PEN (FOR THE PERSON RECEIVING YOUR SIGNALS)

 DRAW A DIAGONAL LINE FROM THE TOP RIGHT-HAND CORNER TO THE BOTTOM LEFT-HAND CORNER OF EACH YELLOW SHEET OF PAPER. CUT ALONG THE LINES. GLUE EACH TRIANGLE ONTO THE BACKS AND FRONTS OF THE RED PAPERS, MAKING SURE THE RED TRIANGLES ARE ALWAYS AT THE TOP.

 PLACE THE ADHESIVE TAPE ALONG THE LEFT-HAND EDGE OF EACH FLAG, HALF ON THE PAPER AND HALF OFF.

 PLACE THE DOWEL OVER THE TAPE, LINING IT UP WITH THE TOP OF THE FLAG. FLIP OVER THE FLAG AND PULL THE TAPE TIGHT, ROLLING THE PAPER AROUND THE DOWEL AS YOU GO. PRESS HARD TO MAKE SURE THE TAPE STICKS TO BOTH DOWEL AND THE PAPER.

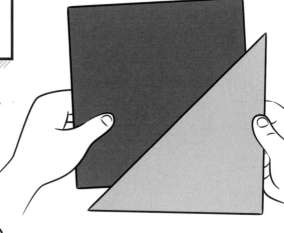

 USE THE ALPHABET OPPOSITE TO PRACTISE A FEW WORDS THAT YOU'D LIKE TO SIGNAL. LEND THIS BOOK TO YOUR MATES SO THEY CAN READ YOUR SIGNALS. YOU CAN STAND AS FAR AWAY FROM THEM AS YOU LIKE, AS LONG AS THEY CAN STILL SEE YOUR FLAGS!

DID YOU KNOW?
The semaphore flag system was designed over 150 years ago for signalling ships at sea.

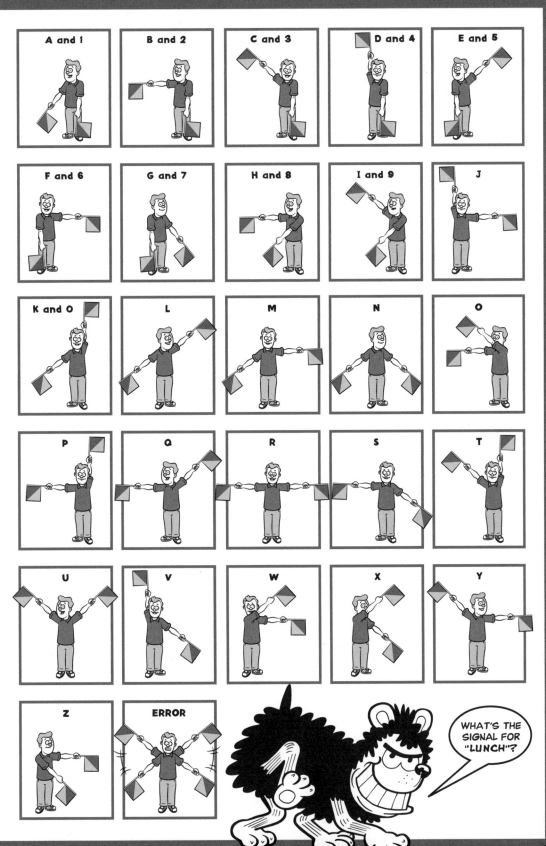

GUSHING GEYSER

With just a few simple items, you can create a mighty gushing geyser. How high can you shoot yours up into the air?

YOU WILL NEED:

- A BOTTLE OF COLA OR DIET COLA (2 LITRES WORKS WELL)
- A PACKET OF MINT-FLAVOURED MENTOS SWEETS
- A FUNNEL (OPTIONAL)
- A HELPFUL ADULT

 1 FIND AN OPEN SPACE OUTDOORS WHERE YOU CAN REALLY MAKE A BIG MESS. YOU'LL NEED PLENTY OF ROOM SO YOU DON'T GET ALL STICKY AND YUCKY!

 2 STAND THE BOTTLE OF COLA UPRIGHT AND UNSCREW THE LID. IF YOU HAVE A FUNNEL, PUT IT INTO THE TOP OF THE BOTTLE.

 3 ASK AN ADULT TO DROP ABOUT HALF A PACKET OF MENTOS INTO THE BOTTLE THROUGH THE FUNNEL AND QUICKLY GET OUT OF THE WAY! STAND FAR BACK TO WATCH A MIGHTY, BUBBLING GEYSER ERUPT FROM THE BOTTLE. WHOOSH!

GLUB! ER... HAS ANYONE GOT A TOWEL I CAN USE?

TOP TIP:

Make sure that the cola bottle is at room temperature. Regular cola doesn't work as well as diet cola!

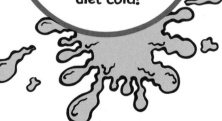

MAKE A SUPER
STRING TELEPHONE

Don't want your teacher to know what you're chatting about? Just have a sneaky chat with this string-powered phone!

YOU WILL NEED:

- 2 PAPER CUPS
- 30 METRES OF NON-STRETCHABLE THREAD (KITE STRING OR FISHING LINE)
- MEASURING TAPE OR RULER
- SEWING NEEDLE
- AN ADULT AND A FRIEND

 CUT A LONG LENGTH OF STRING, BETWEEN 20 AND 30 METRES LONG. ASK AN ADULT TO HELP YOU MAKE HOLES IN THE MIDDLE OF THE BOTTOM OF YOUR CUPS WITH A SEWING NEEDLE. THREAD THE STRING THROUGH EACH CUP AND TIE A KNOT AT EACH END, INSIDE THE CUPS.

 TAKE ONE OF THE CUPS EACH AND SPREAD APART UNTIL THE STRING IS TIGHT. ONE OF YOU SHOULD TALK INTO THE CUP WHILE THE OTHER ONE LISTENS. CAN YOU HEAR WHAT YOUR MATE IS SAYING?

WHEN DOESN'T A TELEPHONE WORK UNDERWATER?

WHEN IT'S "WRINGING" WET!

DID YOU KNOW?

Sound waves travel better through solids (such as your cup and string) than through air, letting you hear sounds that are much further away!

LAUNCH A
VINEGAR ROCKET

Bicarbonate of soda and vinegar make brilliant rocket fuel. Mix them together in an empty drinks bottle to launch your own rocket!

YOU WILL NEED:
- 1 EMPTY PLASTIC BOTTLE
- 1 PIECE OF WHITE TISSUE
- 1 CORK
- 3 PENCILS
- STICKY TAPE
- BICARBONATE OF SODA
- VINEGAR
- SAFETY GOGGLES

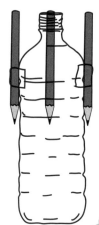

1 TAPE THE PENCILS TO THE SIDE OF THE BOTTLE IN A TRIANGLE TO MAKE FINS. THE BOTTOM ENDS OF THE PENCILS SHOULD BE FACING UPWARDS AND THEY SHOULD ALSO LINE UP AT THE TOP OF THE BOTTLE.

2 PUT TWO LARGE SPOONFULS OF BICARBONATE OF SODA INTO THE MIDDLE OF THE TISSUE. FOLD THE CORNERS UP AND TWIST TO HOLD THE POWDER INSIDE.

3 FILL THE BOTTLE ABOUT A THIRD OF THE WAY UP WITH VINEGAR.

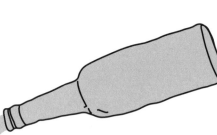

AWESOME PLAYING, GNASHER!

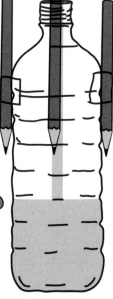

GNEE-HEE! WE REALLY ROCK IT!

4 MAKE SURE YOU'RE OUTSIDE BEFORE YOU DO THIS NEXT STEP! PUSH THE BICARBONATE OF SODA PARCEL INTO THE TOP OF THE BOTTLE. YOU MAY NEED AN ADULT TO HELP YOU PUSH THE CORK FIRMLY INTO THE TOP OF THE BOTTLE.

5 GENTLY SHAKE THE BOTTLE, MAKING SURE YOU KEEP IT AWAY FROM YOUR FACE. QUICKLY STAND THE ROCKET UP ON ITS FINS AND MOVE AWAY!

6 STAND WELL BACK AND WAIT FOR BLAST-OFF!

WELL, IT'S BEEN A BLAST, BUT I'VE GOTTA RUN!

SAFETY FIRST!
Always do this with an adult. Stay well away from the bottle. You **MUST** be outdoors in a large space!

BUILD A BIRDBRAINED
BIRD FEEDER

You could feed your feathered friends, then train them to become your very own flying attack squadron!

YOU WILL NEED:

- PINE CONE
- BIRDSEED
- PEANUT BUTTER
- STRING
- SCISSORS
- BUTTER KNIFE
- BOWL

 CUT A LENGTH OF STRING AND TIE IT TO THE TOP OF THE PINE CONE.

 PUT THE BIRDSEED AND ANY EXTRAS (SUCH AS SUNFLOWER SEEDS, CORN OR NUTS) INTO A BOWL. SPREAD PEANUT BUTTER OVER THE CONE.

 DIP THE STICKY CONE INTO YOUR BOWL OF SEED. NOW ROLL IT AROUND UNTIL THE PEANUT BUTTER IS COMPLETELY COVERED WITH SEEDS.

ASK AN ADULT TO HELP YOU HANG THE CONE FROM A TREE BRANCH OR UP HIGH. MAKE SURE ANIMALS THAT LIKE TO EAT BIRDS CAN'T REACH IT!

THIS TASTY WORM BURGER IS GOING TO BE A REAL "TWEET"!

BECOME A
WEATHER WIZARD

Planning a day of mischief and need to know what the weather is going to be like? Here's an easy way to predict the weather!

YOU WILL NEED:
- A LARGE PINE CONE
- A PAPER STRAW
- SCISSORS
- GLUE

1 CUT OFF THE TOP OF A FLEXIBLE STRAW AT THE END WHERE IT BENDS.

2 PLACE THE TIP OF THE STRAW ON TOP OF AN OPEN SCALE OF THE PINE CONE. GLUE INTO PLACE.

I RECKON IT'S GOING TO RAIN TOMATOES!

3 PUT YOUR PINE CONE ONTO A WINDOWSILL. WHEN THE AIR IS HUMID, THE SCALES OF THE PINE CONE WILL CLOSE AND THE STRAW WILL RISE. THAT MEANS IT'S LIKELY TO RAIN. WHEN IT'S SUNNY, THE SCALES OPEN UP AND THE STRAW BENDS DOWN. IT'S JUST LIKE MAGIC!

BUILD A
BUG HOTEL

Make a "hotel" for bugs to shelter in during the cold winter months, then show them to your mates to see which ones gross them out!

YOU WILL NEED:
- LARGE PLASTIC BOTTLES
- SCISSORS
- CORRUGATED CARD
- STRAW, DRY LEAVES, SMALL TWIGS, MOSS OR BARK
- FELTING OR PLASTIC SHEET
- A HELPFUL ADULT

1 GET SOME LARGE PLASTIC SODA BOTTLES AND REMOVE ANY LABELS. ASK AN ADULT TO HELP YOU TO CUT OFF THE BOTTOMS WITH A PAIR OF SCISSORS. KEEP THE TOPS SCREWED ON.

2 LINE EACH PLASTIC BOTTLE WITH CORRUGATED CARD. THIS WILL MAKE IT DARK INSIDE THE BOTTLE, SPOOKY!

3 FILL EACH BOTTLE WITH NESTING MATERIALS LIKE STRAW, DRY LEAVES, SMALL TWIGS, MOSS AND BARK. PACK THEM IN AS TIGHTLY AS POSSIBLE SO THEY DON'T FALL OUT.

4 STACK THE BOTTLES INTO A PYRAMID SHAPE AND COVER THEM WITH FELTING OR PLASTIC. WEIGH THE "ROOF" DOWN WITH LOGS OR TENT PEGS SO THAT IT DOESN'T BLOW AWAY. CHECK YOUR HOTEL REGULARLY TO MAKE SURE THAT IT'S INTACT, AS WELL AS TO SPOT VISITORS!

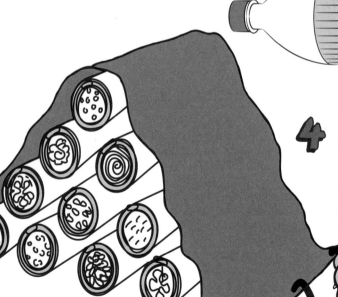

I HOPE IT'S GOT A BUG LOO!

Go on a bug hunt and see if you can spot these bugs in your garden or on nearby parkland.

THIS SPIDER WILL COME IN HANDY!

✔ **Grasshopper**

✔ **Dragonfly**

✔ **Butterfly**

✔ **Beetle**

✔ **Bee**

✔ **Ant**

✔ **Spider**

✔ **Woodlouse**

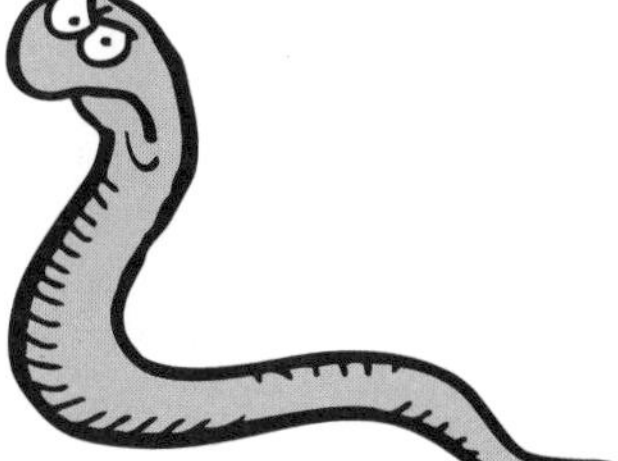

TRICK OR TRUNK

Find out how old any tree is by using this handy trick. Even your teachers aren't this clever!

 1 FIND A TREE THAT YOU WANT TO KNOW THE AGE OF. WRAP A TAPE MEASURE AROUND THE TRUNK AND MEASURE ITS CIRCUMFERENCE (OR GIRTH).

DID YOU KNOW?
The oldest tree in the world is over 5000 years old? That's even older than your dad!

 2

IF YOU'VE MEASURED IN CENTIMETRES, DIVIDE BY 2.5. IF YOU'VE MEASURED IN INCHES, DIVIDE THIS FIGURE BY ONE. THE GROWTH OF AN AVERAGE TREE GIRTH PER YEAR IS 2.5 CM OR 1 INCH. SO A TREE WITH A 40 CM (16 INCH) GIRTH WILL BE ABOUT 16 YEARS OLD!

$$\frac{40\text{IN}}{1} = 40 \text{ YEARS OLD}$$

If you know the species of a tree, you can age it more accurately. For example, oaks and beeches grow approximately 1.75 cm per year. Pine trees grow about 3 cm per year and sycamores grow around 2.75 cm per year. Divide by these figures instead of 2.5.

Beech

Sycamore

Oak

Pine

WHERE'S THE TREE? I NEED A WEE!

MAKE A BARMY
BIRD BATH

No one likes having a bath, but even stinky old birds need to clean their feathers sometimes!

YOU WILL NEED:

- PLANT POT OR BUCKET
- SAUCER (IDEALLY WITH A ROUGH SURFACE)
- GARDEN PAINT
- WATERPROOF GLUE OR TILE ADHESIVE
- PEBBLES
- WATER

1 FIND AN OLD PLANT POT OR BUCKET. TURN IT UPSIDE DOWN AND PAINT IT WITH ALL KINDS OF CRAZY COLOURS, PATTERNS AND PICTURES!

2 NOW PAINT THE SAUCER. TRY TO USE ONE WITH A ROUGH SURFACE FOR THE BIRDS' FEET TO GRIP WITHOUT SLIPPING. TERRACOTTA PLANT SAUCERS ARE PERFECT. LEAVE BOTH THE POT AND THE SAUCER TO DRY OVERNIGHT.

3 GLUE AROUND THE TOP OF THE UPTURNED POT. PLACE THE SAUCER ON TOP, MAKING SURE THAT IT'S POSITIONED IN THE MIDDLE. PRESS FIRMLY AND ALLOW THE GLUE TO SET.

GRR! BEA HATE BATH TIME!

4 FIND A SAFE PLACE TO PUT YOUR BIRD BATH. NEARBY BRANCHES ARE USEFUL FOR BIRDS TO HOP TO SAFETY FROM A SWOOPING BIRD OF PREY OR A HUNGRY CAT!

5 PILE SOME PEBBLES ON ONE SIDE OF THE SAUCER FOR THE BIRDS TO PERCH ON. THEY WILL ALSO PROVIDE A SPOT FOR INSECTS TO LAZE AROUND IN THE SUN.

6 FILL THE SAUCER WITH WATER, MAKING SURE THE PEBBLES ARE SLIGHTLY ABOVE THE WATERLINE TO MAKE A PERCH. PASSING BIRDS NOW HAVE A PERFECT SPOT FOR A DIP OR DRINK!

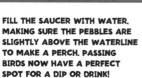

SQUAWK! WHO'S PINCHED MY BUBBLE BATH?

TOP TIP:
Set up a wildlife camera to record your visitors. You can note which birds come to visit during different times of the year!

STARRY SPOTTER

Did you know? There are at least 88 different constellations of stars, each named after animals or characters from mythology? Wowzers!

TOP TIP:
Find out when you can see a meteor shower near you and spot a shooting star!

WHERE ARE YOU?

The biggest constellation is called Orion, also known as The Great Hunter. How can you find it? Go outside in the evening and look at the south-west sky if you are in the northern hemisphere, or the north-western sky if you are in the southern hemisphere. If you live on or near the equator, Orion is visible in the western sky.

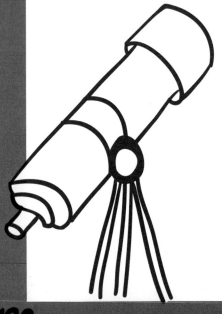

URSA MAJOR

A famous constellation is Ursa Major or the Great Bear. Inside Ursa Major is the Plough, also called the Big Dipper. But guess what? The Plough is NOT a constellation. It's actually called an "asterism", which is a grouping of stars within a larger constellation.

ORION

Look for the pattern of stars shown here. Three bright stars close together in a line are easiest to spot first. These three stars represent Orion's Belt. Two bright stars above this are Orion's shoulders. The two below are actually his knees!

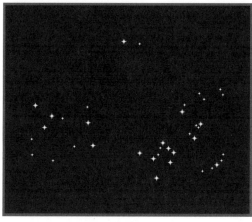

CANIS MAJOR

Near Orion you may be able to see Canis Major and Canis Minor, Orion's two hunting dog pals!

I'M ABOUT TO CAUSE SOME MAJOR TROUBLE!

SUPER-SPEEDY
SCAVENGER HUNT

Get your mates round to your house, hide a load of old items and see who can find the most the fastest. GO FOR IT!

I'M ALWAYS ON THE HUNT FOR MORE NANAS!

WHERE TO PLAY

Your back garden or a local park are perfect places to hold a scavenger hunt, but it works indoors, too! Once you've chosen a place to play, make sure everyone knows where they should be looking and not to go outside that area. Always make sure that an adult knows where you are, if your hunt is outside your home.

MAKE A LIST

Start by coming up with a list of things for players to find. Here are a few great ideas:

ON AN OUTDOOR SCAVENGER HUNT:
- PINE CONE
- FLOWER
- LEAF LARGER THAN YOUR HAND
- LEAF SMALLER THAN YOUR PALM
- SOMETHING THAT SMELLS STINKY
- ROUND OBJECT
- FEATHER
- PIECE OF BARK
- TWIG SHAPED LIKE A "Y"

ON AN INDOOR SCAVENGER HUNT:
- TOOTHBRUSH
- BOOK
- DVD
- CUSHION
- TOILET ROLL
- SPOON
- ODD SOCK
- RUBBER DUCK
- CLOTHES PEG

SECRET ITEMS!
Hide funny items (like an egg cup or a toy) around the search area. Tell your players that whoever finds these bonus items gets a special bonus prize, like a yummy biscuit!

I ALWAYS WIN!

NO. 1

THE WINNER IS...
The first person to collect all the items on their list is the winner. When everyone comes back, take a good look at your collection to see what loot you've found!

SPLAT SPUDZOOKA

This potato cannon uses the awesome power of air pressure to send your enemies scarpering... SPLAT, SPLAT, SPLAT!

YOU WILL NEED:

- A LENGTH OF COPPER PIPING, 30–60 CM
- DOWEL OR BAMBOO CANE
- LARGE RAW POTATO
- METAL NAIL FILE
- AN ADULT TO HELP YOU

 1 FIND A LENGTH OF COPPER PIPING. IF YOU DON'T HAVE ANY, ASK FOR AN OFF-CUT AT YOUR LOCAL DIY STORE. THEY MAY CUT IT TO SIZE FOR YOU, TOO. OTHERWISE, ASK AN ADULT TO CUT IT TO BETWEEN 30 AND 60 CM LONG.

 2 MAKE SURE THE PIPE IS STRAIGHT AND THE ENDS ARE SMOOTH. IF THERE ARE ANY ROUGH EDGES, ASK AN ADULT TO FILE THEM DOWN FOR YOU. DO NOT TOUCH THE ENDS BEFORE THEY ARE FILED DOWN, AS THEY MAY CUT YOU. OUCH!

 3 TIME TO "LOAD" YOUR SPUDZOOKA! PUT THE POTATO ONTO A TABLE (MAKE SURE YOU PROTECT THE TABLE FIRST) AND HOLD IT WITH ONE HAND. WITH THE OTHER HAND, PUSH ONE END OF THE PIPE ALL THE WAY THROUGH THE POTATO.

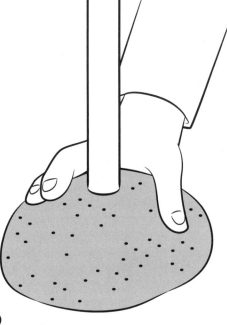

I'M OFF TO PINCH ALL OF MUM'S SPUDS NOW!

DID YOU KNOW?

Air pressure can be really, REALLY powerful. It's even been used to launch satellites into space. **Amazing!**

4 PUSH THE OTHER END OF THE PIPE THROUGH A DIFFERENT PART OF THE POTATO IN THE SAME WAY AS BEFORE. TAKE THE PIPE OUT. NOW YOU SHOULD HAVE POTATO INSIDE BOTH ENDS OF THE PIPING.

5 LINE THE PIPE UP AND AIM AT A TARGET. POKE ONE END OF YOUR SPUDZOOKA WITH THE DOWEL AND KEEP POKING UNTIL IT "FIRES".

6 NEVER FIRE YOUR SPUDZOOKA AT PEOPLE OR ANIMALS. IT'S ALWAYS BEST TO BE OUTDOORS IN A LARGE SPACE WHEN YOU'RE SPLATTING.

7 TO USE YOUR SPUDZOOKA AGAIN, PUSH THE POTATO OUT THAT'S STILL THERE WITH YOUR DOWEL AND RELOAD, AS IN STEPS 3 AND 4. SPLAT ATTACK!

TOP TIP:
Try splatting the outside wall of your house as quickly as you can, then run inside *before your parents see who did it!*

MAKE A TRICKY
STICK TRAIL

Head for your local woodland or park and lay a tricky trail for your mates to follow. Also handy for leading enemies into a trap!

YOU WILL NEED:
- BUCKET
- STICKS, STONES AND OTHER NATURAL OBJECTS (FOUND ON THE GROUND)
- A FEW FRIENDS

 1 GATHER SOME STICKS, STONES, PINE CONES, FEATHERS, LEAVES AND ANY OTHER NATURAL OBJECTS YOU CAN FIND. PLACE THEM IN A BUCKET. ONLY TAKE DEAD THINGS FROM THE GROUND!

 2 DECIDE ON WHERE YOUR TRACK STARTS AND FINISHES AND LAY TRAILS ALONG THE ROUTE. YOU CAN MAKE UP YOUR OWN SYMBOLS OR USE SOME OF THE EXAMPLES BELOW.

 3 NOW IT'S TIME FOR YOUR FRIENDS TO TRACK YOU DOWN! USE A FEW STICKS TO SHOW THEM WHAT TO LOOK OUT FOR AND WHAT YOUR SYMBOLS MEAN. ASK THEM TO COUNT TO 100 WHILE YOU RACE TO THE END OF YOUR TRAIL AND HIDE. CAN THEY FOLLOW YOUR TRAIL TO FIND YOU? WILL ENEMIES FALL INTO YOUR TRAP?

SAFETY FIRST!
Always tell your parents where you're going!

Go straight on

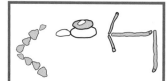

Turn left

Turn right

Wrong way

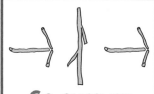

Go over an obstacle

Follow the stream

MAKE YOUR OWN BEANO
BOOMERANG

When I throw stuff away, I don't really want it to come back – but this awesome boomerang is just perfect for chucking!

YOU WILL NEED:
- THIN CARD
- PENCIL
- SCISSORS

 1 TAKE A THIN SHEET OF CARD AND COPY THE BOOMERANG SHAPE BELOW ONTO IT. CUT IT OUT AND FOLD DOWN EACH OF THE THREE EDGES ALONG THE DOTTED LINES.

 2 NOW DRAW YOUR FAVOURITE BEANO CHARACTERS ONTO YOUR BOOMERANG. LOOKING GOOD!

 3 TO THROW YOUR BOOMERANG, HOLD IT BY ONE OF THE WINGS, WITH THE UNFOLDED EDGE FACING FORWARDS. BRING YOUR ARM FORWARDS IN A SWINGING MOTION AND LET GO. THEN WAIT FOR IT TO COME BACK... LOOK OUT!

139

ARE YOU AN ALPHA BRAIN?

Wow your mates, parents and teachers by showing them you can find letters in all sorts of weird and wacky places!

YOU WILL NEED:
- CAMERA OR PHONE
- PINE CONES, PAPER CLIPS, PENS
- A FEW FRIENDS

1 GO FOR A WALK IN YOUR NEIGHBOURHOOD TO BEGIN A LETTER HUNT. ALWAYS TAKE AN ADULT WITH YOU OR LET ONE KNOW WHERE YOU'RE GOING. LOOK FOR LETTERS ON SIGNS, STORES AND CARS. WHEN YOU SEE A LETTER THAT YOU LIKE THE LOOK OF, TAKE A PHOTO OF IT.

2 NOW LOOK FOR LESS OBVIOUS LETTERS. THERE ARE LOTS OF SHAPES IN BUILDINGS, PLANTS AND ALL SORTS OF OBJECTS THAT LOOK LIKE DIFFERENT LETTERS. THE LETTER "E" MIGHT BE HALF A WINDOW FRAME OR A GATE, A SET OF TRAFFIC LIGHTS OR THE SHADOW OF SOME TELEPHONE LINES.

3 NOW TRY MAKING YOUR OWN LETTERS! YOU COULD TRACE THEM IN THE SAND OR THE EARTH, OR YOU MIGHT LAY THEM OUT WITH LEAVES AND PINE CONES, OR PAPER CLIPS AND PENS. YOU COULD EVEN ASK A FRIEND TO MAKE THE SHAPE OF A LETTER WITH THEIR BODY!

4 TRY TO COLLECT THE WHOLE ALPHABET AND THEN PRINT THEM OUT TO WRITE SECRET MESSAGES TO YOUR MATES. THEY'RE GREAT FOR MAKING FUNNY BIRTHDAY CARDS, TOO!

LOOK AT ME! I'M AN "X"!

MAKE CRAZY
STICK
CREATURES

If you're bored in the park, you can have tons of fun making these freaky stick beings!

YOU WILL NEED:

- STICKS (FOUND ON THE GROUND)
- THREAD OR PIPE CLEANERS
- GOOGLY EYES
- GLUE
- MARKER PENS
- BITS OF FABRIC
- SCISSORS

1 PICK OUT A GOOD-LOOKING STICK, AND DECIDE WHAT TO USE FOR ITS BODY. USE THREAD OR PIPE CLEANERS TO TIE ON SMALLER TWIGS FOR ARMS AND LEGS.

2 KNOBBLY BITS COULD BE THEIR OPEN MOUTHS OR LIPS. STICK ON GOOGLY EYES AND USE MARKER PENS TO DRAW SOME FUNNY FACES!

3 WRAP PIECES OF FABRIC AROUND YOUR STICK CREATIONS FOR CLOTHES. GIVE THEM A SCARF, HAT, T-SHIRT AND EVEN PANTS!

TOP TIP:

Play a silly game by pretending one of the sticks smells yucky and chase after your mates with it!

TIME TO PLAY FETCH!

MAKE A MUCKY
MUD FACE

After a rain shower, there's plenty of mud around. It's the perfect time to create a Menacing mud face. Let's get mucky!

YOU WILL NEED:

- MUD
- WATER
- BUCKET
- SPADE OR TROWEL
- NATURAL THINGS LIKE PINE CONES, FERN LEAVES AND MOSS.

1 DIG UP SOME MUD AND PUT IT IN A BUCKET. THE STICKIER THE MUD IS, THE BETTER. ADD WATER TO MAKE IT EVEN STICKIER IF YOU NEED TO!

2 MAKE A MUD BALL IN YOUR HANDS AND SQUASH IT ONTO A TREE TRUNK, SHAPING IT INTO A FACE.

3 USE NATURAL MATERIALS TO ADD FEATURES TO YOUR MUD FACE LIKE EYES, TEETH, A MOUTH, A NOSE, HAIR AND EVEN HORNS!

4 GIVE YOUR CREATION A NAME AND LEAVE IT FOR SOMEONE ELSE TO FIND. WHEN YOU GO BACK, MAYBE ANOTHER FACE WILL HAVE APPEARED NEXT TO IT!

MINE IS A SELF-PORTRAIT!

5 IF YOU'VE GOT ENOUGH MUD LEFT OVER, YOU COULD TRY MAKING MUD FACES OF ALL THE MENACING MATES!

CREATE YOUR OWN
MINI LEAF BOAT

Try making these amazing mini leaf boats with your mates, then race them in a stream to see who has the fastest!

YOU WILL NEED:
- A PIECE OF BARK
- TWIG
- LARGE LEAF
- SOME WATER TO SAIL ON

1 COLLECT YOUR MATERIALS. YOU WILL NEED A GOOD-SIZED PIECE OF BARK THAT IS FLAT AND BROAD ENOUGH TO FORM THE HULL OF YOUR BOAT. IF THERE'S NO BARK ON THE GROUND, YOU COULD PEEL IT AWAY FROM A FALLEN, ROTTING TREE TRUNK, BUT NEVER A LIVE TREE!

2 MAKE A SMALL HOLE IN THE BARK WITH A TWIG. TRY TO GET THE HOLE AS CENTRAL AS POSSIBLE AND PUSH A TWIG INTO IT. IT NEEDS TO FIT SNUGLY. THIS WILL BE YOUR MAST.

3 THREAD A BIG LEAF OR A SERIES OF LEAVES ONTO THE STICK FOR A SAIL. NOW FIND SOME WATER AND GET READY TO SET SAIL!

ER... DOES ANYONE KNOW HOW TO SAIL THIS THING?

TOP TIP:
Find a small pebble and place it on the hull or on top of the mast. You could even decorate the pebbles to look like Beano characters!

HOW TO TALK TO
GNASHER!

Gnasher says a lot more than just "Gnash, Gnash," y'know. Here's a handy guide on how to speak Gnashese!

GNICE
Translation: Nice!
Gnasher says this when he sees a juicy-looking bone!

GNOPE
Translation: Nope!
What Gnasher says when someone tries to make him take a bath!

GNOPE! THERE'S GNOTHING AS GNICE AS A GNUMMY GNAWESOME BONE TO GNOSH! GNA-HA!

GNUM

Translation: Yum!
Gnasher yells this when he
sees a plate of SAUSAGES!

GNAWESOME

Translation: Awesome!
Everything that Dennis
does is GNAWESOME!

GNOSH

Translation: Food!
Sausages! Bones! Pizza!
Anything is Gnosh to Gnasher!

GNA-HA!

Translation: Ha ha!
Gnasher laughs like this when
Dennis gives Walter a wedgie!

SPORTS & GAMES

Feeling sporty? If you want to keep fit AND have loads of fun with your friends, then check out all these brilliant Beano sports, great games and awesome activities!

POOH STICKS

Play this game with your mates the next time you cross a bridge over a stream. Whoever has the fastest stick will become the Pooh champ!

YOU WILL NEED:
- 2 OR MORE STICKS
- A STREAM
- A BRIDGE

1 EACH OF YOU NEEDS TO FIND A STICK. YOU COULD TIE A PIECE OF DIFFERENT-COLOURED STRING TO EACH STICK TO REMIND YOU WHICH ONE IS YOURS.

2 GATHER ON THE SIDE OF THE BRIDGE WHERE THE STREAM RUNS IN (UPSTREAM) STAND SIDE BY SIDE, HOLDING YOUR STICKS AT ARM'S LENGTH OVER THE STREAM.

3 READY, STEADY, GO! QUICKLY DROP YOUR STICKS AT THE SAME TIME.

4 RUN TO THE OTHER SIDE OF THE BRIDGE (DOWNSTREAM). IF YOUR STICK APPEARS FIRST, YOU'RE THE WINNER!

I'M OFF TO CHECK MY STICK!

EGG-AND-SPOON RACE

Ever been in an egg-and-spoon race? Grab your friends to race against or compete against the clock to become an egg-spert!

YOU WILL NEED:

- ENOUGH EGGS FOR EACH OF YOUR COMPETITORS
- SPOONS TO BALANCE THE EGGS ON
- STICKS OR ROPES
- AN ADULT TO HELP YOU

1 HARD-BOIL THE EGGS IN WATER FOR ABOUT 8 MINUTES SO THEY'RE HARD. ALLOW THEM TO COOL DOWN BEFORE YOU USE THEM. IT'S BEST TO HAVE AN ADULT AROUND FOR THIS STEP!

I'VE GOT PRANK PLANS FOR THIS EGG ONCE I WIN THE RACE!

2 DECIDE ON YOUR RACECOURSE, AND MARK THE START AND FINISH LINES WITH ROPES OR STICKS. PICK OUT A SPOON THAT'S BIG ENOUGH TO FIT YOUR EGG ON IT, BUT NOT TOO BIG THAT THE EGG ROLLS AROUND!

3 HOLD ONE ARM OUT IN FRONT OF YOU, WITH THE EGG AND SPOON ALMOST AT EYE HEIGHT. KEEP YOUR HEAD AND ARM AS STILL AS YOU POSSIBLY CAN, WHILE RUNNING AS SMOOTHLY AS YOU POSSIBLY CAN. AVOID ANY SUDDEN MOVEMENTS! KEEP YOUR EYE ON THE FINISH LINE AND TRY NOT TO DROP YOUR EGG. IF YOU DROP YOUR EGG, YOU HAVE TO GO BACK TO THE BEGINNING!

DESIGN A BEANO
BOARD GAME

Making your own awesome Beano board game is easier than you think – and best of all, you get to make up your own rules!

YOU WILL NEED:

- A LARGE PIECE OF PAPER (OR 2 SHEETS STUCK TOGETHER)
- COLOURED PENCILS, PENS AND PAINTS
- COUNTERS AND DICE
- A PIECE OF BOARD FOR YOUR FINISHED GAME

1 THE AIM OF A BOARD GAME IS USUALLY TO TRAVEL FROM ONE END OF A PATH TO THE OTHER. SKETCH THE PATH ON THE PAPER, STARTING IN ONE CORNER. HAVE A ROUND NUMBER OF SQUARES, E.G. 50 OR 80.

2 YOU'LL NEED SOME LEAPS FORWARD AND SETBACKS ALONG THE WAY, SO ADD A FEW ARROWS SHOWING WHERE PLAYERS MIGHT JUMP AHEAD OR GO BACK ON THE BOARD.

3 THINK OF A THEME – FOR EXAMPLE, SOME EXPLORERS ARE LOST IN THE JUNGLE AND HAVE TO FIND THEIR WAY OUT. THIS WILL HELP YOU TO DESIGN THE BOARD, AND COME UP WITH REWARDS AND TRICKS TO SUIT THE STORY.

I'M GOING TO NEED NANA POWER TO BEAT DOCTOR GLOOM!

4 YOU COULD INCLUDE CARDS FOR PLAYERS TO PICK UP. IF SO, ADD SOME "PICK UP A CARD" SQUARES AND WRITE INSTRUCTIONS ON THE CARDS, E.G. "TIGER AHEAD! HIDE AND MISS A TURN."

5 WRITE INSTRUCTIONS IN THE SQUARES WHERE PLAYERS HAVE TO MOVE FORWARDS AND BACKWARDS, SUCH AS "CLIMB UP A JUNGLE VINE TO 35".

6 TEST OUT YOUR GAME BY PLAYING IT WITH FRIENDS. IF IT WORKS WELL, COPY IT ONTO A PIECE OF BOARD AND DESIGN A COOL BACKGROUND. OTHERWISE, MAKE A FEW TWEAKS AND TRY IT OUT AGAIN. EASY!

I NEED TO SEARCH FOR WAYS TO CHEAT!

HOT POTATO!

This is a super sneaky game to play on a long, boring car journey!

YOU WILL NEED:
- A SMALL OBJECT
- A FRIEND

1 CHOOSE AN OBJECT THAT YOU CAN HIDE IN SOMEONE'S BAG OR POCKET. IT SHOULD BE SOMETHING EASY TO GUESS. A SMALL TOY IS A GOOD CHOICE, OR A STINKY OLD SOCK. THIS OBJECT IS THE "HOT POTATO"!

2 THE IDEA IS TO PASS THE HOT POTATO ON WITHOUT SOMEONE KNOWING THEY'RE GETTING IT. YOU COULD POP IT IN THEIR POCKET OR BAG. WHEN THEY DISCOVER IT, THEY MUST ADMIT THEY'VE GOT IT AND SNEAKILY PLOT TO PASS IT ON AGAIN!

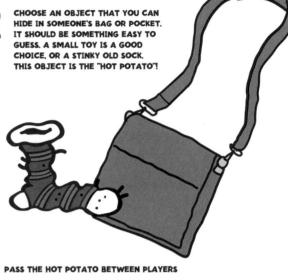

3 PASS THE HOT POTATO BETWEEN PLAYERS THROUGHOUT YOUR TRIP. WHO WILL DISCOVER THEY HAVE IT WHEN YOU ALL GET HOME?

4 IF ANYONE SEES YOU HIDING THE HOT POTATO, YOU HAVE TO TAKE IT BACK AND TRY AGAIN!

I BET SHE'LL SMELL DENNIS'S STINKY SOCK BEFORE SHE SEES IT!

WATER BALLOON
VOLLEYBALL

Ah, the perfect game to play on a hot day at the beach, in the park or even in your back garden. But watch out – you're going to get **WET**!

YOU WILL NEED:
- A NET
- WATER BALLOONS
- WATER
- 2 TOWELS

1 SET UP YOUR NET AND GATHER TOGETHER SOME PLAYERS. YOU'LL NEED AT LEAST FOUR PEOPLE TO PLAY THIS GAME.

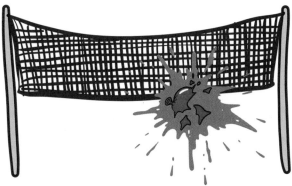

2 GET A PILE OF WATER BALLOONS READY.

3 EACH TEAM GRABS A BEACH TOWEL OR BLANKET AND USES IT TO LAUNCH A BALLOON OVER THE NET FOR THE OTHER TEAM, WHO HAVE TO TRY TO CATCH IT IN THEIR TOWEL. THE WINNING TEAM IS THE ONE THAT BURSTS THE FEWEST BALLOONS – AND STAYS THE DRIEST!

TOP TIP:
Double the fun: try playing with *two water balloons* at the same time!

HOW TO
PRO
BODYBOARD

Learning to bodyboard is loads of fun! You'll soon be pulling off all sorts of awesome tricks to impress your mates. Wipe out!

YOU WILL NEED:
- WAVES
- SUNBLOCK
- BODYBOARD
- LEASH
- WETSUIT (IT NEEDS TO FIT SNUGLY BUT STILL ALLOW MOVEMENT)
- BOOTIES
- FINS (A WETSUIT, BOOTIES AND FINS CAN USUALLY BE HIRED AT THE SAME TIME A BODYBOARD)

1 WATCH SOMEONE ELSE BODYBOARD FIRST TO GET THE IDEA. THEN PRACTISE ON THE BEACH, USING YOUR FEET AND ARMS TO PADDLE. THIS WILL GIVE YOU A NICE WARM-UP, TOO!

2 NOW IT'S TIME TO GET INTO THE WATER! MAKE SURE YOU'RE WEARING YOUR SAFETY LEASH. LIE FLAT ON YOUR BELLY, HOLDING THE SIDE OF THE BOARD WITH YOUR HANDS. KEEP YOUR SHOULDERS PARALLEL TO YOUR HANDS, WITH YOUR ELBOWS BENT, RESTING CLOSE TO THE OUTER EDGE OF THE BOARD. KICK YOUR FEET, KEEPING THEM UNDERWATER.

3 KICK AND PADDLE TO WHERE THE WAVES ARE BREAKING. CHOOSE THE WAVE YOU WANT TO RIDE, STARTING WITH A SMALL ONE. A FEW SECONDS BEFORE THE WAVE STARTS TO BREAK, POINT THE NOSE OF YOUR BOARD TOWARDS THE BEACH.

DON'T PANIC!
If you fall off your board, keep calm – pull on your leash until you get hold of it again. Your board will keep you afloat!

4 JUST AS THE WAVE REACHES YOU, PUSH OFF TOWARDS THE SHORE. LET THE BOARD TAKE YOUR WEIGHT AND LEAN UP ON YOUR ELBOWS, WITH YOUR HEAD UP AND YOUR BACK ARCHED.

TOP TIP:
Make sure that you have the right sized board. They range from 90 to 115 cm long. Stand the board upright. It should come up to your belly button or to about 2 cm on either side of it. So if you're 120 cm tall, then your bodyboard would be 90 cm long!

SAFETY FIRST!
The beach can be very dangerous if you're not careful. Always take an adult with you and do not try to boogie board unless you are a good swimmer. Always make sure that you don't go too far out, so you won't get caught in a strong ocean current!

5 IF YOU'VE CAUGHT THE WAVE, IT'LL TAKE YOU ALL THE WAY TO THE BEACH. AND THE BEST BIT? YOU GET TO GO BACK IN AGAIN AND AGAIN!

SURF'S UP, GNASHER!

THIS IS GNARLY!

155

CLOBBER
ROBBERS

This is a great game to play with your mates and you won't even get into trouble for pinching things for a change!

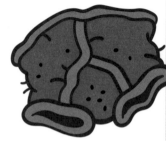

YOU WILL NEED:
- 4 LARGE CARDBOARD BOXES
- 2 MATCHING SETS OF DRESSING-UP CLOTHES, BIG ENOUGH TO FIT ALL PLAYERS (SHIRTS, SHORTS, JACKETS, HATS, SCARVES OR TIES, GLOVES)

 1 PUT TWO BOXES CONTAINING THE SAME ITEMS OF CLOTHES AT ONE END OF A ROOM AND TWO EMPTY BOXES AT THE OTHER END. DIVIDE THE PLAYERS INTO TWO TEAMS. GET HALF OF EACH TEAM TO LINE UP NEXT TO THE EMPTY BOXES AND HALF NEXT TO THE FULL BOXES.

 2 ON THE WORD "GO", TWO OF THE PLAYERS STANDING NEXT TO THE EMPTY BOXES RACE TO THEIR TEAM'S BOX OF CLOTHES. THEY MUST STEAL THEM, PUT THEM ALL ON, RACE BACK TO THE EMPTY BOX, THEN TAKE OFF THE CLOTHES AND PUT THEM IN THE EMPTY BOX!

 3 THE PLAYERS STANDING AT THE OPPOSITE END (BY THE EMPTY BOXES) THEN TAKE A TURN AND SO ON. THE FIRST TEAM TO FINISH, ONCE EVERYONE HAS HAD A TURN, IS THE WINNER!

WHAT'S IN THE BIG BAG?

Grab a group of friends and family members of different ages and play this totally brilliant game!

YOU WILL NEED:
- A CLOTH BAG
- A COLLECTION OF EVERYDAY OBJECTS

 1 ONE PLAYER PUTS SOMETHING INTO THE BAG WITHOUT SHOWING THE OTHERS. HE HE!

 2 THE OTHERS HAVE TO GUESS WHAT'S IN THE BAG JUST BY FEELING AROUND INSIDE IT. DON'T PUT ANYTHING SHARP IN THERE, BUT IT CAN BE YUCKY OR STICKY!

 3 THE FIRST PLAYER TO GUESS CORRECTLY GETS A POINT. THEN THE NEXT PLAYER CHOOSES SOMETHING TO GO IN THE BAG. THE FIRST PLAYER TO GET FIVE POINTS WINS THE GAME!

4 ONCE YOU'VE FINISHED, TRY PLAYING AGAIN, BUT THIS TIME SEE WHO CAN COME UP WITH THE BEST SILLY STORY, JUST BY USING ALL OF THE ITEMS IN THE BAG!

COOL BIKE TRICKS

Impress your friends by mastering these awesome bike tricks! Remember to wear a helmet, in case you fall off, and safety pads help, too.

YOU WILL NEED:
- A BIKE
- PROTECTIVE GEAR SUCH AS A HELMET, KNEE PADS AND ELBOW PADS ARE ESSENTIAL

BUNNY HOP

 START BY PUSHING FORWARDS SLOWLY. GET READY TO PULL THE FRONT OF THE BIKE UP.

 PULL THE FRONT WHEEL UP. AS IT STARTS TO MOVE BACK TOWARDS THE GROUND, USE YOUR LEGS TO KICK THE FRONT OF THE BIKE UP.

 WITH BOTH OF THE BIKE WHEELS OFF THE GROUND, YOU CAN HOP OVER OBSTACLES!

 FOR A SMOOTH LANDING, BEND YOUR ARMS AND KNEES AS YOU LAND BACK ON THE GROUND. YOU SHOULD ALWAYS TRY TO LAND ON THE BACK WHEEL OR BOTH WHEELS.

POP A WHEELIE

 1 PRACTISE ON GRASS AND MAKE SURE YOU WEAR A HELMET AND SAFETY PADS. YOU WANT TO STAY SAFE!

 2 PUT YOUR SEAT DOWN A BIT, SO YOU'RE SITTING LOW ON YOUR BIKE. IF YOUR BIKE HAS GEARS, PUT IT IN FIRST TO START OFF.

 3 START TO PEDAL AS SLOWLY AS YOU CAN WITHOUT FALLING OFF! TRY TO KEEP YOUR FEET ON THE PEDALS.

 4 GET YOUR PEDALS TO ELEVEN O'CLOCK AND FIVE O'CLOCK. PUSH DOWN ON THE ELEVEN O'CLOCK PEDAL.

 5 NOW PUSH DOWN ON THE HANDLEBARS AND THEN IMMEDIATELY WHIP THE BARS UP. THIS WILL BRING THE FRONT WHEEL UP.

6 LEAN BACK A LITTLE (BUT NOT TOO MUCH) AND YOU SHOULD FIND YOURSELF RIDING ON THE BACK WHEEL. PRACTISE YOUR BALANCE AND YOU'LL SOON BE POPPING WHEELIES LIKE A PRO!

ALIEN INVASION
SKITTLE CHALLENGE

Try defeating these pesky alien invaders by bowling them over!

YOU WILL NEED:

- 6 OR 10 SMALL PLASTIC BOTTLES (ALL THE SAME SIZE) WITH LIDS
- GOOGLY EYES
- ACRYLIC PAINTS
- WHITE CARD
- SCISSORS
- BLACK MARKER PEN
- GLUE
- A LIGHT BALL
- NEWSPAPER TO PROTECT YOUR WORK SURFACE

1 SPREAD OUT SOME NEWSPAPER, THEN POUR A SMALL AMOUNT OF PAINT INTO EACH PLASTIC BOTTLE. PUT THE LIDS ON TIGHTLY AND SWIRL THE PAINT AROUND UNTIL THE BOTTLES ARE FULLY COVERED.

2 DRAW SOME COOL ALIEN SHAPES THE SIZE OF THE BOTTLES ONTO WHITE CARD AND PAINT THE SHAPES TO MATCH THE BOTTLES.

3 ASK AN ADULT TO HELP YOU CUT OUT THE ALIENS SHAPES. YOU COULD ALSO ADD SOME GOOGLY EYES, CUT OUT FROM ANY SPARE CARD.

160

4 STICK THE EYES ONTO THE ALIENS AND USE THE BLACK MARKER TO ADD THE PUPILS. DRAW A MOUTH FOR EACH ALIEN.

5 STICK THE ALIEN SHAPES ONTO THE MATCHING COLOURED BOTTLES AND LEAVE THE GLUE TO DRY.

6 ARRANGE THE SKITTLES IN A TRIANGLE SHAPE AT ONE END OF A ROOM. NOW ROLL THE BALL ALONG THE FLOOR AND TRY TO KNOCK OVER AS MANY ALIEN SKITTLES AS YOU CAN! WHO WILL KNOCK THE MOST OVER AND SAVE THE PLANET?

C'MON, GNASHER, LET'S GO **BLAST** THOSE ALIENS!

TOP TIP:
You could stick numbers on the back of each alien **and** award points for each skittle knocked down!

161

GLOW-IN-THE-DARK
RING TOSS

Here's a totally awesome game that'll really test your throwing skills. You also get to play it at night! How good is your aim?

YOU WILL NEED:

- 6 CLEAN 500 ML PLASTIC DRINKS BOTTLES WITH SCREW TOPS (TALL JAM JARS WITH LIDS ALSO WORK)
- WATER
- LARGE PACKET OF 30 CM GLOW STICKS, INCLUDING CONNECTORS
- 6 GLOW STICKS 15 CM LONG FOR PUTTING INSIDE THE BOTTLES

1 WAIT UNTIL IT GETS DARK. FILL EACH BOTTLE THREE-QUARTERS FULL WITH WATER. BEND AND SHAKE SIX SMALLER GLOW STICKS TO ACTIVATE THEM. DROP ONE INTO EACH BOTTLE. SCREW ON THE BOTTLE TOPS.

2 EACH PLAYER TAKES 5 TO 10 OF THE LONGER GLOW STICKS AND CONNECTORS, MAKING THEM INTO RINGS. BEND AND SHAKE THEM TO ACTIVATE THEIR GLOW!

3 SET THE BOTTLES ABOUT 30 CM APART, IN A TRIANGLE SHAPE. DECIDE ON YOUR THROWING LINE AND ALL STAND BEHIND IT.

4 TAKE IT IN TURNS TO THROW YOUR RINGS, TO GET AS MANY POINTS AS POSSIBLE. YOU GET THREE POINTS FOR EACH RING THAT LANDS OVER A BOTTLE AND ONE POINT FOR A RING THAT TOUCHES A BOTTLE. REMEMBER TO KEEP BEHIND THE THROWING LINE!

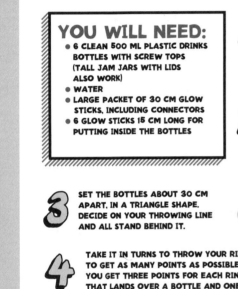

GNE-HEE! I CAN DO THIS WITH **MY EYES** CLOSED!

HOW TO BE A SUPER
FOOTY
STRIKER!

Ever dreamed of scoring goals like Cristiano Ronaldo? It'll take a lot of practice if you want to become a superstar striker!

YOU WILL NEED:
- A STURDY WALL
- CHALK
- SOFT BALL

1 CHALK GOALPOSTS ONTO A WALL AT DIFFERENT HEIGHTS AND WIDTHS. MARK THE SCORES ONTO THE WALL – WRITE 10 POINTS FOR THE EASIEST, 50 POINTS FOR THE HARDEST AND SO ON.

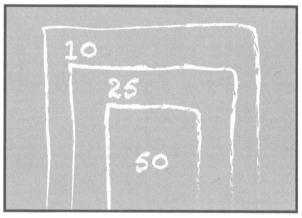

2 MARK A KICK LINE TO PLACE THE BALL ON. AIM AT THE GOALPOSTS TO SCORE POINTS. CHALK YOUR POINTS ON THE PAVEMENT.

3 AFTER 10 KICKS, ADD UP YOUR SCORES. HOW DID YOU DO? TAKE ANOTHER 10 KICKS AND SEE IF YOU CAN BEAT YOUR ORIGINAL SCORE. PLAY WITH MATES TO SEE WHO'S THE BEST!

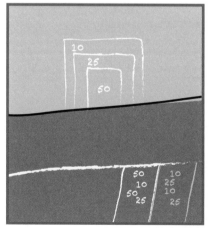

TRY AND **DODGE** THIS VOLLEY!

4 NOW TRY SHOOTING AGAIN, BUT THIS TIME SEE WHO CAN SCORE THE MOST POINTS THE FASTEST!

BATTLING BATTLESHIPS

Before you go on a long trip or holiday, why not make some battleship grids on scrap paper to take with you? FIRE!

YOU WILL NEED:
- A4 SCRAP PAPER AND PENS
- RULER
- ENVELOPE TO STORE YOUR GRIDS

1 DRAW SOME GRIDS USING A RULER AND PEN. DRAW TWO GRIDS ON ONE A4 SHEET OF PAPER TO MAKE A SET. EACH GRID SHOULD BE 10 SQUARES ACROSS AND 10 SQUARES DOWN. YOU DON'T HAVE TO BE TOO ACCURATE ABOUT THE SQUARE SIZE!

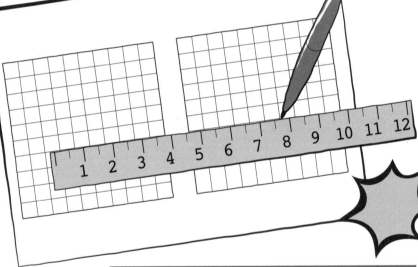

2 NUMBER THE GRIDS – FROM 1 TO 10 ACROSS THE TOP AND FROM A TO J DOWN THE SIDE.

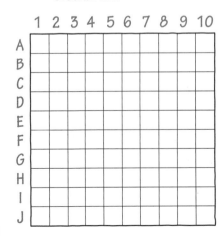

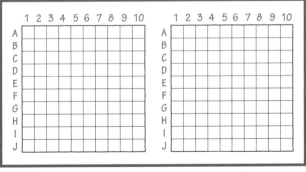

3 EACH PLAYER GETS A SET OF TWO GRIDS. THEY MARK THEIR FLEET OF BATTLESHIPS ON THE FIRST GRID. PLACE YOUR SHIPS ANYWHERE ON THAT GRID, GOING UP OR ACROSS (BUT NOT DIAGONALLY).

SAND DARTS

Are you a devil on the dartboard, like me? Try this version the next time you're on a beach!

YOU WILL NEED:
- SAND
- PEBBLES AND SHELLS

1 COLLECT A PILE OF SMALL PEBBLES AND SHELLS. THESE WILL BE YOUR "DARTS". AVOID LARGE AND HEAVY PEBBLES OR ROCKS THAT COULD HURT SOMEONE BY MISTAKE!

2 USE YOUR FINGER OR ONE OF THE PEBBLES TO DRAW A SMALL CIRCLE IN THE SAND, ABOUT THE WIDTH OF YOUR FOOT. DRAW FOUR BIGGER CIRCLES AROUND THAT CIRCLE.

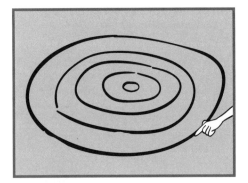

3 MARK THE CIRCLES WITH THE POINTS YOU CAN EARN FOR EACH RING: 10, 20, 30, 40 AND 50 (FOR THE BULLSEYE IN THE CENTRE). DRAW A LINE IN THE SAND TO STAND BEHIND FOR EACH THROW.

4 TAKE TURNS THROWING YOUR SAND DARTS INTO THE RING. ALWAYS THROW UNDERARM. KEEP SCORES IN THE SAND AND PLAY TO WIN!

I'VE GOT MY SAND DARTS, NOW I WANT A SANDWICH!

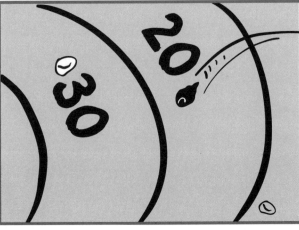

DOCTOR, DOCTOR!

This is a hilarious game to play and it works best with at least six friends.

YOU WILL NEED:
● AT LEAST 6 FRIENDS

1 PLAYERS SHOULD STAND SHOULDER TO SHOULDER IN A CIRCLE. EACH PLAYER THEN GRABS THE HAND OF TWO DIFFERENT PEOPLE ON THE OPPOSITE SIDE OF THEM.

2 NOW PLAYERS HAVE TO TRY TO UNTANGLE THE KNOT, WITHOUT LETTING GO OF EACH OTHER'S HANDS, BY STEPPING OVER OR UNDER ARMS! THEY NEED TO END UP STANDING IN A CIRCLE AGAIN. SOME PLAYERS MAY NOW BE FACING OUTWARDS.

3 TO MAKE THE GAME EASIER, START WITH EVERYONE IN A CIRCLE HOLDING HANDS, THEN ASK SOME OF THEM TO CROSS THEIR ARMS AND HOLD THEIR NEIGHBOURS' HANDS. IT'S REALLY TRICKY!

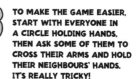

TOP TIP:
If the knot is impossible to untangle, players can agree to release one pair of hands!

167

CRAZY CONKERS

This is a really old game that your mum and dad probably played when they were kids. Why not give it a try and perhaps you can beat your parents at their own game!

YOU WILL NEED:
- A CONKER
- DRILL
- SHOELACE OR STRING
- AN ADULT

1 FIRST, FIND SOME SUITABLE CONKERS. GENERALLY, THE BIGGER, THE BETTER. AVOID THE ONES WITH WHITE SPOTS ON THEM – THEY'RE RUBBISH!

2 ONCE YOU'VE FOUND A GOOD CONKER, YOU'LL NEED AN ADULT TO MAKE A HOLE FROM THE TOP, ALL THE WAY THROUGH. THEY COULD USE A SHARP OBJECT FOR THIS (SUCH AS A NAIL), BUT THERE'S A RISK OF THE CONKER CRACKING. INSTEAD, ASK THEM TO DRILL A SMALL HOLE THROUGH IT.

3 NOW FIND YOUR STURDIEST SPARE SHOELACE. GUIDE THIS THROUGH THE HOLE AND TIE A STRONG KNOT AT ONE END, TO STOP THE CONKER SLIDING STRAIGHT OFF. YOU'LL LIKELY NEED THREE OF FOUR KNOTS TO MAKE SURE IT'S STRONG ENOUGH.

IF YOU THINK YOU CAN BEAT ME AT THIS GAME, YOU MUST BE CONKERS!

Now you're ready for some serious conker battling!

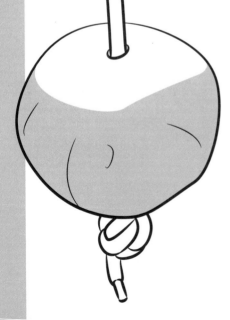

HOW TO PLAY

1 WRAP THE SHOELACE AROUND YOUR HAND, ENSURING YOU HAVE A STRONG GRIP ON IT. WHEN IT'S YOUR TURN, HOLD THE STRING UNDER THE PART HOLDING THE CONKER WITH TWO FINGERS. TAKE AIM AND HIT THE OTHER CONKER WITH YOURS AS HARD AS YOU CAN!

2 WHEN IT'S YOUR OPPONENT'S TURN, LET YOUR CONKER DANGLE DOWN ON ITS STRING. BE CAREFUL NOT TO LET IT DANGLE TOO LOW OR YOU ARE AT RISK OF IT WINDMILLING. THIS IS WHEN THE CONKER SPINS IN A COMPLETE CIRCLE. IF THIS HAPPENS THEN YOUR OPPONENT GETS ANOTHER GO.

3 CAN YOU DESTROY YOUR OPPONENT'S CONKER BEFORE THEY DESTROY YOURS? GO FOR IT!

THIS GAME IS TOTALLY SMASHING!

ULTIMATE TRAY
MEMORY GAME

Show your teachers you're a real brainbox by playing this great game. Try the handy memory trick below to see if it improves your score!

YOU WILL NEED:
- A TRAY OR LARGE PLATE
- 10–20 SMALL EVERYDAY OBJECTS (SUCH AS A COMB, A PENCIL SHARPENER, A COIN, A SPOON)
- A CLOTH TO COVER THE TRAY
- PENCILS AND PAPER

1 TAKE IT IN TURNS TO PUT OBJECTS ON THE TRAY, THEN COVER THEM UP WITH THE CLOTH. REMOVE THE CLOTH AND GIVE EVERYONE ONE MINUTE TO REMEMBER AS MANY ITEMS AS POSSIBLE. IT'S TRICKY!

2 AFTER A MINUTE, COVER UP THE TRAY AGAIN AND ASK THE PLAYERS TO WRITE DOWN ALL THE ITEMS THEY CAN REMEMBER. HOW WELL DID THEY DO? NOW CHANGE THE OBJECTS AND KEEP PRACTISING!

HERE'S A COOL TRICK TO HELP YOU REMEMBER EVERYTHING ON THE TRAY:

IMAGINE YOU'RE GETTING UP TO GO TO SCHOOL AND PLACE EACH OF THE ITEMS ALONG THE WAY.

FOR EXAMPLE, YOU GET UP AND "OUCH!" YOU TREAD ON THE PENCIL SHARPENER. THEN YOU GO INTO THE BATHROOM AND COMB YOUR HAIR.

YOU EAT YOUR BREAKFAST WITH THE SPOON, THEN GET ON THE BUS AND PAY WITH A COIN AND SO ON, UNTIL EACH OF THE OBJECTS HAS A PLACE IN YOUR DAILY ROUTINE. IT'S EASY AND FUNNY!

SPIN A BASKETBALL
ON YOUR FINGER

If you've ever wanted to be an All-Star basketball player and impress your mates, here's your chance!

YOU WILL NEED:
- A BASKETBALL
- A FINGER

1 LET A BIT OF AIR OUT OF THE BASKETBALL TO MAKE IT EASIER TO CONTROL.

2 HOLD THE BALL WITH THE SEAMS FACING UP, WITH THE HAND YOU WRITE WITH CLOSE TO YOU AND THE OTHER HAND ON THE SIDE FACING YOU. KEEP YOUR ELBOWS BENT AND TUCKED INTO YOUR SIDES. THE BALL SHOULD BE ABOUT 10 CM FROM YOUR CHIN.

3 NOW GET SPINNING! SNAP BOTH WRISTS TO START THE BALL SPINNING. A SLOWER SPEED IS MUCH BETTER TO START OFF WITH.

4 QUICKLY CATCH THE BALL WITH THE PAD OF YOUR INDEX FINGER – NOT THE VERY TIP. COUNT TO ONE AND THEN TRY AGAIN UNTIL YOU CAN LAST UNTIL YOU COUNT TO TWO, THEN THREE AND SO ON. THIS BUILDS CONTROL!

I'VE GOT A BRILLIANT SPINNING "TIP"!

5 NOW KEEP IT GOING. BEND YOUR FINGER SLIGHTLY TOWARDS YOU AND TRY TO MOVE THE BALL TO YOUR FINGERNAIL. KEEP YOUR ELBOWS TUCKED INTO YOUR BODY ALL THE TIME. START LIGHTLY BATTING THE BALL WITH THE FINGERTIPS OF YOUR OTHER HAND. YOU'LL BE A BASKETBALL SPINNING CHAMPION IN NO TIME!

REAL-LIFE
SPOT THE DIFFERENCE

Holy banana peel! General Blight has swiped a bunch of items from a room, but I don't know which ones. Maybe this game will help...

YOU WILL NEED:
- A ROOM
- LOTS OF REMOVABLE OBJECTS
- 2 FRIENDS

1 ALL OF THE PLAYERS SHOULD TAKE A LOOK AROUND THE ROOM, THEN ONE STAYS BEHIND WHILE THE OTHERS LEAVE. THE REMAINING PLAYER REMOVES THREE OBJECTS. HMM... VERY SNEAKY!

SAFETY FIRST!
Check with an adult before you start moving things or ask an adult to move them for you, then everyone can play the game!

I'M OFF WITH ALL THE MISSING ITEMS!

2 NOW, THE OTHER PLAYERS COME BACK INTO THE ROOM AND HAVE TO LIST ALL OF THE THINGS THAT HAVE BEEN REMOVED. GAH!

MENACE GAMES

Who needs to play outside when you can make a home-made obstacle course? Use stuff from around your house to make yours a real challenge!

YOU WILL NEED:

- SOFT TOYS
- LAUNDRY BASKET
- HULA HOOP
- LARGE BED SHEET
- 2 OR MORE CHAIRS
- SCARF
- ASSORTMENT OF HATS AND COATS

1 TOY TOSS

PUT A LAUNDRY BASKET AT ONE END OF THE ROOM, GRAB AN ARMFUL OF CUDDLY TOYS AND CUSHIONS, AND TRY TO THROW THEM IN. GET THREE OUT OF FIVE IN THE BASKET BEFORE MOVING ON TO THE NEXT STAGE!

2 FUNNY JUMPS

AT THIS STOP ON THE COURSE, EACH PLAYER DOES A SEQUENCE OF JUMPS IN THE AIR. DO A STAR JUMP, A FROG JUMP AND A BUNNY HOP!

3 HULA-PALOOLA

PLACE A HULA HOOP ON THE FLOOR AND JUMP IN AND OUT OF IT 10 TIMES WITH YOUR FEET TOGETHER. HOW FAST CAN YOU JUMP IN AND OUT?

CHECK OUT MY SPECIAL HIGH-FIVE JUMP!

4 TUNNEL TIME

MAKE A TUNNEL USING A BIG SHEET OR QUILT AND SOME CHAIRS. CLIMB THROUGH THE TUNNEL AND THEN BACK AGAIN BEFORE RACING TO THE NEXT STAGE!

5 TIGHTROPE WALK

PLACE A SCARF IN A STRAIGHT LINE ALONG THE FLOOR AND PRETEND YOU'RE A CIRCUS PERFORMER! WALK ACROSS THE SCARF WITHOUT STEPPING OVER THE EDGES AND HOLD YOUR ARMS OUT TO THE SIDE TO HELP YOU BALANCE.

6 HAT'S THE WAY TO DO IT!

GRAB A PILE OF HATS, SCARVES AND GLOVES. EACH PLAYER MUST PUT THEM ALL ON, STRIKE A FUNNY POSE, THEN TAKE THEM ALL OFF AGAIN!

I WIN! I WIN!

FLAP THE FISH

You'll need to be a flippin' fast fish flapper to flap these flippin' fish fast. Blimey, that's a real tongue-twister!

YOU WILL NEED:

- A NEWSPAPER FOR EACH PLAYER
- SCISSORS
- STICKY TAPE
- A FLOOR SPACE OR TABLE TOP AT LEAST 2 M LONG

1 EACH PLAYER NEEDS TO CUT OUT A FISH SHAPE FROM A SHEET OF NEWSPAPER.

2 PLAYERS ROLL THE REST OF THEIR NEWSPAPER UP AND FIX IT IN PLACE WITH STICKY TAPE, THEN PLACE THEIR FISH ON THE STARTING LINE.

3 USE THE ROLLED-UP NEWSPAPER TO CREATE A DRAUGHT BEHIND THE FISH AND FLAP AS FAST AS YOU CAN TO GET YOUR FISH ACROSS THE FINISHING LINE!

DON'T GET IN A FLAP!

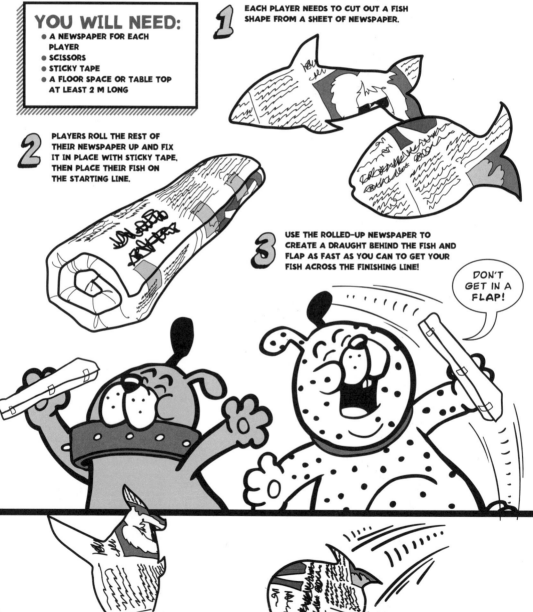

FIND THE FIB

You can let your imagination run wild during this game – but remember, for every cheeky fib, you must tell two truths!

 EACH PLAYER HAS TO GIVE TWO TRUE FACTS AND ONE THAT ISN'T TRUE. FOR EXAMPLE:

"ON MY WAY TO SCHOOL LAST WEEK I SAW A MAN DRESSED AS A BANANA!

IN THE AFTERNOON, I WATCHED A CAT TRYING TO CATCH A FROG AND IT FELL IN A POND.

WHEN I GOT HOME, I FOUND A CHOCOLATE CAKE IN THE FRIDGE!"

 THE OTHER PLAYERS HAVE TO GUESS WHICH FACT HAS BEEN MADE UP. THEY CAN ASK THE STORYTELLER QUESTIONS AND USE THEIR DETECTIVE SKILLS TO REVEAL THE UNTRUTH.

 IF A PLAYER SPOTS THE FIB, THEY GET A POINT. IF ANY PLAYER PICKS THE WRONG FACT, THE STORYTELLER GETS A POINT. GET FIBBING!

YES, CITIZEN, I'M OFF TO SAVE THAT FROG NOW!

HORRIBLE
HOPSCOTCH

It's time to play a classic game of hopscotch, but this time with a twist!

YOU WILL NEED:
- MASKING TAPE
- SCISSORS
- A FLOOR SPACE LARGE ENOUGH FOR AT LEAST 8 SQUARES
- A MARKER, E.G. LARGE BUTTON OR BEAN BAG

1 MAKE A HOPSCOTCH GRID USING MASKING TAPE, AS SHOWN. PLAYERS MUST HOP ON ONE FOOT, EXCEPT WHEN SQUARES ARE SIDE BY SIDE (WHEN THEY CAN PUT A FOOT IN EACH). THEY HAVE TO HOP OVER ANY SQUARE WITH A MARKER IN IT.

2 THE FIRST PLAYER TOSSES THE MARKER INTO SQUARE 1, HOPS OVER SQUARE 1 INTO SQUARE 2, THEN CONTINUES ON TO THE LAST SQUARE. HERE, THE PLAYER TURNS AROUND AND HOPS BACK, STOPPING IN SQUARE 2 TO PICK UP THE MARKER IN SQUARE ONE, THEN HOPPING IN SQUARE 1 AND OUT.

3 THE PLAYER CONTINUES BY TOSSING THE MARKER INTO SQUARE 2 AND SO ON UNTIL THEY MAKE A MISTAKE. THEN THE NEXT PLAYER HAS A TURN.

MINNIE IS GOING TO BE HOPPING MAD WHEN I WIN THIS GAME!

4 A PLAYER IS OUT FOR THAT ROUND IF THE MARKER DOESN'T LAND IN THE RIGHT SQUARE, OR IF THE HOPPER STEPS ON A LINE, GOES INTO A SQUARE WITH A MARKER, PUTS TWO FEET DOWN IN A SINGLE BOX, OR PUTS A SECOND FOOT OR HAND DOWN WHEN PICKING UP THE MARKER. HOP TO IT!

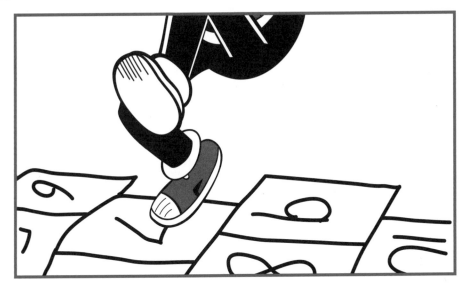

5 TO MAKE THIS GAME EVEN MORE FUN, GET PLAYERS TO DO A FORFEIT IF THEY GET THEIR MARKER IN THE WRONG SQUARE! FOR EXAMPLE, GROWL LIKE A MONSTER, STAND ON ONE LEG, MAKE A MONKEY FACE – WHAT BONKERS IDEAS CAN YOU COME UP WITH?

NOT LIKELY, ROGER. I'M THE HOPSCOTCH QUEEN!

PEBBLE DOMINOES

Check out this great beach domino game. It's been popular since ancient times – a set was even found in Tutankhamun's tomb!

YOU WILL NEED:
- 28 SMOOTH, FLAT STONES
- WHITE PAINT PEN (OR ACRYLIC PAINT, A SMALL BRUSH AND A STEADY HAND)

1 COLLECT 28 SMOOTH, FLAT STONES. WASH THEM TO REMOVE ANY SAND OR SOIL AND PAINT A WHITE LINE ACROSS THE CENTRE OF EACH.

2 ON EITHER SIDE OF THE LINES, MARK TWO SETS OF DOTS IN EVERY COMBINATION FROM ZERO TO SIX. USE THIS HANDY GUIDE SO YOU DON'T MISS ANY!

BOING! BOING! SQUELCH!

3 WHEN THE PAINT IS DRY, PLAY WITH YOUR DOMINOES OUTSIDE OR AT A GARDEN TABLE. YOU'LL NEED AT LEAST ONE OTHER PLAYER. FIRST, PLACE THE DOMINOES FACE DOWN (WITH NO DOTS SHOWING) AND SHUFFLE THEM AROUND. THIS IS THE BONEYARD!

4 EACH PLAYER TAKES SEVEN DOMINOES. THE PLAYERS SHOULD SEE THEIR OWN DOMINOES, BUT NOT THE OTHER PLAYERS'. NO PEEKING! DECIDE WHO STARTS BY EACH PICKING UP A DOMINO FROM THE BONEYARD. THE PLAYER WITH THE HIGHEST NUMBER OF DOTS GOES FIRST.

5 PLACE THE FIRST DOMINO DOWN. THEN THE NEXT PLAYER PLACES ONE OF THEIR DOMINOES AT ONE END OF THE FIRST DOMINO BY MATCHING THE NUMBER OF DOTS. IF THEY CAN'T GO, THEN THEY SHOULD PICK UP A NEW PEBBLE FROM THE BONEYARD.

DO THE SPOTS ON MY BUTT COUNT?

EVIL LEER!

6 THE GAME CONTINUES WITH EACH PLAYER MATCHING ONE END OF THE DOMINO CHAIN IN TURN. IF A DOUBLE IS LAID, SET THE PEBBLE VERTICALLY RATHER THAN HORIZONTALLY. EVERY TIME YOU CAN'T GO, PICK UP A DOMINO FROM THE BONEYARD. IF YOU RUN OUT OF SPACE, START TURNING CORNERS WITH THE PIECES. THE FIRST PLAYER TO USE UP ALL OF THEIR PEBBLES WINS!

TOP TIP:
If a player is caught peeking, they have to do a forfeit - like standing on one leg for their next go!

181

SAY AND CATCH

For this game you need a soft ball, some friends and quick timing. Make sure you stay alert, too!

YOU WILL NEED:
- A SOFT BALL
- SOME FRIENDS

1 FIRST, DECIDE ON A CATEGORY (SUCH AS ANIMALS, POP MUSIC, BEACH, SCHOOL). TO BEGIN THE GAME, ALL PLAYERS HAVE TO STAND IN A CIRCLE, ONE METRE AWAY FROM EACH OTHER.

2 TAKE IT IN TURNS TO THROW THE BALL TO EACH OTHER. BEFORE CATCHING THE BALL, PLAYERS MUST SAY A WORD THAT HAS SOMETHING TO DO WITH THE CHOSEN CATEGORY. SO, IF THE CATEGORY IS ANIMALS, THEY MIGHT SAY "CAT". WORDS CAN ONLY BE USED ONCE, THOUGH!

CAT!

3 ANYONE WHO DROPS THE BALL, CAN'T COME UP WITH A WORD FROM THE CATEGORY OR REPEATS A WORD THAT'S ALREADY BEEN USED IS OUT OF THE GAME!

4 THE LAST PLAYER STANDING IS THE WINNER. NOW, CHOOSE A DIFFERENT CATEGORY FOR A NEW ROUND AND START ALL OVER AGAIN!

I REALLY DROPPED THE BALL ON THAT ONE!

CATCH A FOOTBALL
ON YOUR NECK

If you're having a rubbish football match, pull off this awesome trick. It'll distract the other team long enough for you to grab a scorcher of a goal!

YOU WILL NEED:
- A FOOTBALL
- MATES TO IMPRESS

1 THROW THE BALL STRAIGHT UP IN FRONT OF YOU FROM THE CENTRE OF YOUR BODY. DON'T THROW FORWARDS OR BEHIND. JUST STRAIGHT UP AND NOT TOO HIGH!

2 LOOK STRAIGHT UP AT THE BALL AS IT FALLS AND WATCH IT UNTIL THE LAST POSSIBLE SECOND.

3 WHEN THE BALL IS JUST ABOVE YOU, DUCK YOUR HEAD FORWARDS AND DOWN. AT THE SAME TIME, START LEANING FORWARDS WITH YOUR BODY. YOU'RE AIMING FOR THE BALL TO HIT THE BACK OF YOUR HEAD, JUST ABOVE THE NECK, RATHER THAN YOUR SKULL, WHICH WOULD MAKE THE BALL BOUNCE AWAY.

4 AS SOON AS YOU FEEL THE BALL TOUCH THE TOP OF YOUR NECK, TILT YOUR HEAD BACKWARDS AND HUNCH YOUR SHOULDERS UP. THIS WILL MAKE A SMALL POCKET BETWEEN YOUR SHOULDERS FOR THE BALL TO SIT IN.

WOW!

AND NOW TO GET IT IN THE **BACK** OF THE NET!

OLLIE LIKE DENNIS

One of the coolest skateboarding tricks you can do is a jump called an Ollie. Remember to wear a helmet when using your skateboard!

YOU WILL NEED:
- A SKATEBOARD
- HELMET, KNEE AND ELBOW PADS

SKATEBOARD PARTS:

NOSE

TRUCK

WHEEL

DECK

KICKTAIL

 1 BEND YOUR KNEES. AS YOU ROLL ALONG THE GROUND (SLOWLY!), SLAM YOUR RIGHT FOOT DOWN AS HARD AS YOU CAN ON THE KICKTAIL AND THEN JUMP INTO THE AIR (ABOVE THE SKATEBOARD) WITH BOTH FEET.

 2 AS YOU GO UP INTO THE AIR, DRAG YOUR LEFT FOOT UP THE DECK. IT WILL TAKE TIME AND PRACTICE TO GET THE FEEL FOR THIS, SO KEEP TRYING.

3 BEND YOUR KNEES AS YOU COME DOWN TO SOFTEN THE IMPACT. SOON, YOU WILL BE PULLING OFF MEGA AWESOME OLLIES EVERYWHERE YOU SKATE!

HOW TO STAGE A SPOOKY
HAUNTING!

Have you ever wanted to scare your mates silly? Here's how to make them believe they've really seen a spook, spectre or ghost!

YOU WILL NEED:
- A NOTEPAD AND PEN
- BAKING TRAY, SHEET, SPOOKY ITEMS
- A CAMERA

1 FIRST, MAKE A LIST AND GET ALL OF THE ITEMS READY THAT YOU'LL NEED TO SET UP YOUR HAUNTED HOUSE. YOU MIGHT NEED TO TEST OUT SOME OF THE TRICKS BEFORE YOU INVITE YOUR MATES ROUND AT NIGHT!

2 TRY LEAVING A WINDOW OPEN, SO THAT THE BREEZE BLOWS THE CURTAINS. SHAKE A BAKING TRAY TO MAKE A WEIRD NOISE OR WEAR A SHEET OVER YOUR HEAD AND PRETEND TO BE A CREEPY GHOST!

SERIOUS SPOOKS!

EDINBURGH, SCOTLAND
The famous Edinburgh Playhouse has a friendly ghost called Albert who wears a grey coat. He's believed to be an old stagehand who can't resist helping out now and then!

BANGHAR FORT, INDIA
People say a wizard put a curse on this Indian village and soon after that, the place was invaded. To this day, people there think that the ghosts keep nosy visitors away.

THE CHARLES BRIDGE, PRAGUE
In the Middle Ages, 10 Lords were beheaded on the bridge. Their ghosts still linger on there, singing in the night to scare off anyone who dares to cross the bridge. Spooky!

HELP! I'M TRAPPED UNDER THIS SHEET!

3 WHEN YOUR FRIENDS COME ROUND, TURN OFF ALL THE LIGHTS AND ASK THEM TO EXPLORE YOUR SPOOKY HOUSE. IF ANY OF YOUR TRICKS NEED YOU TO BE IN THAT ROOM, MAKE SURE YOU HIDE IN THERE FIRST BEFORE THEY GET THERE!

JEEPERS! I THINK I SAW A REAL-LIFE GHOST!!

SAFETY FIRST! Clear away any items that your mates might bump into as they're stumbling around in the dark!

TOP TIP: Tell your mates to bring a camera and see if they can capture any spooky goings-on!

THUMB WRESTLER

Here's a chance for you and your mates to battle it out - with your thumbs! Who'll become the all-time thumb wrestling champion?

1 PLACE YOUR THUMBS IN MID-AIR, FACING EACH OTHER. LOCK YOUR FINGERTIPS TOGETHER.

2 BOW YOUR THUMBS, TO RESPECT YOUR OPPONENT. THEN LET THE EPIC WRESTLING MATCH BEGIN!

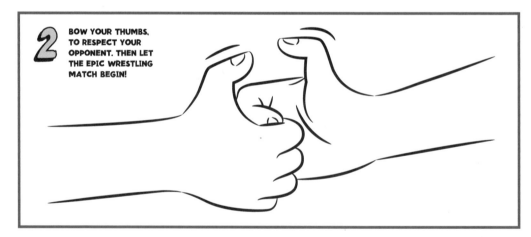

3 THE AIM IS TO TRY TO PUSH YOUR OPPONENT'S THUMB DOWN AND HOLD IT THERE FOR A COUNT OF FIVE.

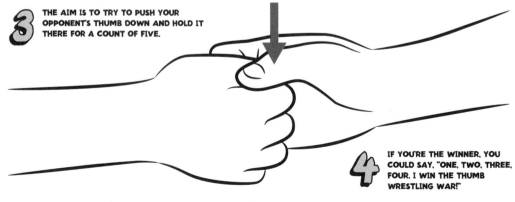

4 IF YOU'RE THE WINNER, YOU COULD SAY, "ONE, TWO, THREE, FOUR, I WIN THE THUMB WRESTLING WAR!"

DROP CATCH

Can you catch a ball on two knees, with one hand on the floor or even with both eyes closed?!

YOU WILL NEED:
- A SOFT BALL
- SOME FRIENDS

1 STAND IN A CIRCLE WITH SOME FRIENDS AND SPACE YOURSELVES OUT EVENLY. THE FURTHER APART YOU ARE, THE MORE CHALLENGING THE GAME WILL BE! DECIDE WHO IS GOING TO START AND GIVE THAT PERSON THE BALL.

2 THE FIRST PERSON SHOULD THROW THE BALL TO ANOTHER PLAYER IN THE CIRCLE. IF THAT PLAYER CATCHES IT, THEY THEN THROW IT TO ANOTHER PLAYER AND SO ON.

3 THE BALL IS THROWN BACK AND FORTH IN THE CIRCLE UNTIL SOMEONE DROPS IT. THE "DROPPER" HAS TO PAY A PENALTY AND CONTINUE TO PLAY ON ONE KNEE. ANY OTHER "DROPPERS" PAY THE SAME PENALTY.

4 IF PLAYERS ON ONE KNEE CATCH THEIR NEXT BALL, THEY CAN STAND BACK UP AGAIN. BUT IF THEY DROP THAT ONE, TOO, THEY PAY ANOTHER PENALTY AND GO DOWN ON TWO KNEES. ON A THIRD DROP, THE PLAYER ON TWO KNEES SHOULD ALSO PUT ONE HAND TO THE GROUND; ON A FOURTH DROP, CLOSE ONE EYE; AND ON A FIFTH DROP, CLOSE BOTH EYES!

5 IF PLAYERS WITH PENALTIES CATCH THE BALL AGAIN, THEY CAN REMOVE ONE PENALTY – FOR EXAMPLE, IF THEY'RE ON TWO KNEES, ONE KNEE CAN COME UP AGAIN. THE LAST PLAYER STILL IN THE GAME IS THE WINNER!

> I CAN CATCH IT ON ALL FOURS WITH MY EYES SHUT!

TRICKY DICKY'S
TOP PRANKS

Try these wicked tricks and cheeky pranks out on your mum and dad!

Sprinkle sugar on your head and start scratching. Your mum will have a look at your head and think you have the worst case of dandruff she's ever seen!

Make cookies with curry powder in the mixture and put them in the cookie jar. Yuck!

Put curlers in your dad's hair while he's sleeping. When he wakes up he'll wonder why everyone's laughing!

Hide a cuddly toy that talks when it's moved inside someone's pillow!

Cover the window with black paper so when your parents wake up, they'll be bamboozled that it's still dark!

Take a pizza out of its box and hide it. Eat one slice and put the crust back in the box, so everyone thinks you ate it all!

Scrape out the filling in all the biscuits in the jar and replace with toothpaste. That's the way the cookie crumbles, Dad!

Fill a cup with water and dried peas. Hide it under your victim's bed. Put it on top of a metal tray that's raised on top of a book. At night, the peas will expand and jump out of the cup onto the tray, making a weird tapping sound that'll freak out the person trying to sleep!

Push a penny onto your forehead until it sticks. Tap the back of your head and it'll fall off. Bet your dad he can't do the same. Push the penny onto his forehead, but don't leave it on there. Hide it in your hand. He'll think it's on his forehead and keep hitting his head trying to knock it off!

Make fake chocolate chip cookies! Mix kidney beans into mashed potato and ask your mum to bake them for ten minutes until they go golden brown. Leave them out for your hungry dad to find!

Turn a packet of biscuits into a giant elastic band ball by wrapping loads round it. It'll take anyone ages to unravel it and get to the cookies!

Switch rooms and beds with your sister or brother right before your mum comes to wake you up. When they pull back the covers, they'll freak out!

Put a piece of thick rope underneath the sheet at the bottom of your mum and dad's bed. When they get into bed, their feet will touch it and they'll think it's a snake.

Only do this to someone with a real sense of humour. Put a few crisps in the toes of their slippers to give them the jeepers creepers!

Ask an adult to take an old metal tape measure apart and roll up the tape into a tight circle. Put one end between the edge of a drawer and then close it. When someone opens the drawer, it'll spring out and scare them!

Cut a hole underneath a pizza box, big enough for your hand to fit through. Cover the hole with the pizza. When your dad takes a slice, push your hand through and quickly grab it back!

Change the mouse settings on your dad's computer so that up is down and down is up! How long will it take him to work out what you've done?

Cover the middle part of a sunflower with pepper and see how many people you can get to sniff it and sneeze. Ahchoo!

PRANKS FOR ALL THE LAFFS, MUM AND DAD!

Ring the doorbell and pretend to answer it. Shout to your dad and pretend there's a pizza delivery guy at the door with 20 pizzas and he wants paying!